OECD *Economic Surveys*
Electronic Books

The OECD, recognising the strategic role of electronic publishing, will be issuing the OECD *Economic Surveys*, both for the Member countries and for countries of Central and Eastern Europe covered by the Organisation's Centre for Co-operation with Economies in Transition, as electronic books with effect from the 1994/1995 series -- incorporating the text, tables and figures of the printed version. The information will appear on screen in an identical format, including the use of colour in graphs.

The electronic book, which retains the quality and readability of the printed version throughout, will enable readers to take advantage of the new tools that the ACROBAT software (included on the diskette) provides by offering the following benefits:

❑ User-friendly and intuitive interface
❑ Comprehensive index for rapid text retrieval, including a table of contents, as well as a list of numbered tables and figures
❑ Rapid browse and search facilities
❑ Zoom facility for magnifying graphics or for increasing page size for easy readability
❑ Cut and paste capabilities
❑ Printing facility
❑ Reduced volume for easy filing/portability

Working environment: DOS, Windows or Macintosh.

Subscription: FF 1 800   US$317   £200   DM 545

Single issue: FF 130   US$24   £14   DM 40

Complete 1994/1995 series on CD-ROM:

FF 2 000   US$365   £220   DM 600

Please send your order to OECD Electronic Editions or, preferably, to the Centre or bookshop with whom you placed your initial order for this Economic Survey.

OECD
ECONOMIC
SURVEYS

1994-1995

CANADA

ORGANISATION FOR ECONOMIC CO-OPERATION AND DEVELOPMENT

ORGANISATION FOR ECONOMIC CO-OPERATION AND DEVELOPMENT

Pursuant to Article 1 of the Convention signed in Paris on 14th December 1960, and which came into force on 30th September 1961, the Organisation for Economic Co-operation and Development (OECD) shall promote policies designed:

— to achieve the highest sustainable economic growth and employment and a rising standard of living in Member countries, while maintaining financial stability, and thus to contribute to the development of the world economy;

— to contribute to sound economic expansion in Member as well as non-member countries in the process of economic development; and

— to contribute to the expansion of world trade on a multilateral, non-discriminatory basis in accordance with international obligations.

The original Member countries of the OECD are Austria, Belgium, Canada, Denmark, France, Germany, Greece, Iceland, Ireland, Italy, Luxembourg, the Netherlands, Norway, Portugal, Spain, Sweden, Switzerland, Turkey, the United Kingdom and the United States. The following countries became Members subsequently through accession at the dates indicated hereafter: Japan (28th April 1964), Finland (28th January 1969), Australia (7th June 1971), New Zealand (29th May 1973) and Mexico (18th May 1994). The Commission of the European Communities takes part in the work of the OECD (Article 13 of the OECD Convention).

Publié également en français.

3 2280 00481 3648

Table of contents

Tables

Figures

BASIC STATISTICS OF CANADA

THE LAND

Area (thousand sq. km)	9 976	Population of major cities, including metropolitan	
Agricultural area (1990, as per cent of total area)	6.4	areas (thousands)	
		Montréal	2 943
		Toronto	3 502

THE PEOPLE

Population (1994)	29 225 000	Civilian labour force (1994)	14 832 000
Number of inhabitants per sq. km	2.9	Employment agriculture (1994)	424 600
Population, annual net natural increase		Immigration (annual average 1990-1994)	234 199
(average 1990-1994)	195 700	Average annual increase in civilian labour force	
Natural increase rate per 1 000 inhabitants		(1990-1994, per cent)	0.9
(average 1990-1994)	7.0		

PRODUCTION

GDP in 1994 (millions of Canadian dollars)	750 053	Origin of gross domestic product (1994, per cent	
GDP per head (Canadian dollars)	25 665	of total, 1986 prices):	
Gross fixed investment (private and public)		Agricultural, forestry and fishing	2.8
per head (Canadian dollars)	4 763	Mining and quarrying	4.3
Gross fixed investment (private and public)		Manufacturing	18.4
as per cent of GDP	18.6	Construction	5.5
		Non business sector	17.4
		Other	54.4

THE GOVERNMENT

		Composition of Parliament (October 1995): (number of seats)	House of Commons	Senate
Government current expenditure on goods and services (1994, as per cent of GDP)	20.1			
Government gross fixed capital formation (1994, as per cent of GDP)	2.2	Progressive Conservative	2	52
		Liberal	178	43
Federal Government current revenue (1994, as per cent of GDP)	18.7	New Democratic	9	–
		Bloc Québecois	53	–
Federal direct and guaranteed debt (1994, per cent of current expenditure)	251.7	Independent	1	2
		Reform	52	–

FOREIGN TRADE

Exports (1994)		Imports (1994)	
Exports of goods and services, as per cent		Imports of goods and services, as per cent	
of GDP	32.2	of GDP	32.5
Main exports (per cent of commodity exports):		Main imports (per cent of commodity imports):	
Wheat	1.6	Industrial materials	17.9
Natural gas	3.0	Motor vehicles and parts	23.6
Lumber and sawmill products	6.3	Producers' equipment	32.3
Pulp and paper	6.9	Consumer goods	11.6
Other metals and minerals	9.6	Main suppliers (per cent of commodity imports):	
Motor vehicles and parts	26.3	United States	74.8
Other manufactured goods	26.8	EEC	7.9
Main customers (per cent of commodity exports):		Japan	4.1
United States	81.7		
EEC	5.2		
Japan	4.3		

THE CURRENCY

Monetary unit: Canadian dollar	Currency unit per US dollar, average of daily figures:	
	Year 1994	1.366

Note: An international comparison of certain basic statistics is given in an annex table.

This Survey is based on the Secretariat's study prepared for the annual review of Canada by the Economic and Development Review Committee on 13 September 1995.

•

After revisions in the light of discussions during the review, final approval of the Survey for publication was given by the Committee on 16 October 1995.

•

The previous Survey of Canada was issued in November 1994.

Introduction

After finally gaining momentum in 1994, the economic recovery in Canada faltered in early 1995, as activity in the United States slowed and tighter domestic monetary conditions moderated domestic demand. As a result, the output gap has widened again and the decline in unemployment has come to a halt. With interest rates easing markedly in recent months, the upturn is projected to have resumed, however, in the second half of 1995. Indeed, interest-sensitive sectors – such as housing and consumer durables – should be stimulated, while strongly improved international competitiveness is likely to limit the damping effect of weaker US demand on Canadian exports. Nonetheless, sustained economic expansion would be greatly assisted by a continued rebalancing of the macroeconomic policy mix towards further fiscal restraint, which should, over time, lead to interest rate levels consistent with the good inflation performance currently being achieved in the country.

With inflation within the official target range, in recent years, the Bank of Canada has in most periods been seeking to ease monetary conditions in order to help close the persistent output gap. Since 1994, however, this has been complicated by rising interest rates in the United States and repeated downward pressure on the Canadian dollar associated with the domestic political and public finance situation. The fiscal problem is due fundamentally to the accumulated stock of public debt. If it were not for debt interest payments, the government budget would already be in surplus, given the consolidation efforts at both the federal and provincial levels. But with a high debt-to-GDP ratio by international comparison, government finances continue to be vulnerable to any economic downswing or interest rate increases. Resulting concerns about the sustainability of Canada's fiscal position underlie recurrent financial market nervousness and downgrades of sovereign debt by major credit rating agencies.

Emphasis on structural policy has been maintained, with the broad aim of enhancing productivity performance. As regards the labour market, a number of changes to the unemployment insurance system have been made, or are being considered, to reduce inherent incentive distortions and ensure budget savings. Industrial policy measures have focused on enhancing competition, particularly through deregulation and privatisation, as well as through the reduction of barriers to internal and international trade; they have also sought to encourage small business growth and research and development.

Chapter I of the Survey examines the main factors underlying recent economic developments, which have been characterised by a dichotomy between foreign and domestic demand, and then discusses the short-term outlook. Chapter II reviews macroeconomic policies, with particular attention given to the implications of high public debt. Chapter III examines progress in structural reform, focusing on the announced overhaul of the unemployment insurance system. Chapter IV contains a special study of Canada's industrial performance, including an assessment of government policies in this area. Conclusions arising from the analysis in the Survey are presented in Chapter V.

I.   Recent trends and short-term prospects

A narrowly-based recovery

Canada's recovery from the recession of the early 1990s was unusually slow and lagged that in the United States. Output and employment regained their pre-recession levels only after two and more than three years, respectively, which is twice as long as following the previous downswing in the early 1980s (Figure 1). The upturn finally gathered momentum in 1994, when real GDP growth, at 4^1/2 per cent, exceeded somewhat that in the United States. But this spurt of activity has proved short-lived, with economic expansion slowing sharply in early 1995, despite a strong build-up of inventories.

The main reason why the recovery has failed to maintain its momentum is that it has remained relatively narrowly-based due to an unbalanced policy mix (see Chapter II). Indeed, the easing of monetary conditions since 1991 has been dominated by a decline in the exchange rate while real interest rates, constrained by persistent fiscal and political concerns, have remained relatively high. As a result, the recovery has mainly relied on foreign demand and – to a lesser extent – business investment. Although in 1994 it showed signs of broadening to the household sector, exports still were the major source of growth, drawing strength from the US expansion and marked depreciation of the Canadian dollar (Figure 1). By contrast, household demand has proved fragile, responding rather quickly and strongly to the run-up in interest rates over the year to early 1995. Growth has also been held back by spending cutbacks in the public sector. The underlying weakness of domestic demand reflects the fact that the Canadian economy has not been able to adequately ''uncouple'' interest rates from those in the United States, despite different ''fundamentals'' in the two countries.

The gradual nature of the recovery has meant that – in contrast to the United States – economic slack has remained substantial, putting downward pressure on

Figure 1. **KEY ASPECTS OF ECONOMIC ACTIVITY**

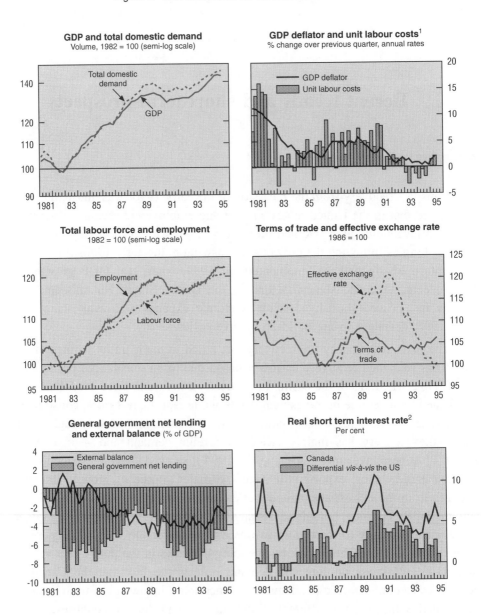

GDP and total domestic demand
Volume, 1982 = 100 (semi-log scale)

Total domestic demand

GDP

GDP deflator and unit labour costs[1]
% change over previous quarter, annual rates

GDP deflator
Unit labour costs

Total labour force and employment
1982 = 100 (semi-log scale)

Employment

Labour force

Terms of trade and effective exchange rate
1986 = 100

Effective exchange rate

Terms of trade

General government net lending and external balance (% of GDP)

External balance
General government net lending

Real short term interest rate[2]
Per cent

Canada
Differential *vis-à-vis* the US

1. Total economy.
2. 90-day commercial paper rate, deflated by the GDP deflator.
Source: CANSIM – Statistics Canada.

Figure 2. **THE OUTPUT GAP**

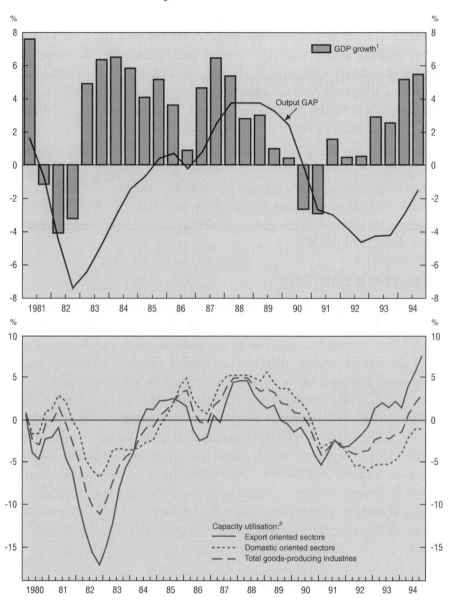

1. Annual rates.
2. Deviation from long term average.
Source: Statistics Canada; Department of Finance; OECD Secretariat.

5

inflation. While, according to OECD Secretariat estimates, in the 1980s the output gap was virtually closed three years from the cyclical trough, it still amounted to 2½ per cent of potential output in the second half of 1994 (Figure 2) and has widened again since. This overall picture conceals, however, sharply diverging sectoral developments. Reflecting the dichotomy of domestic and foreign demand discussed above, capacity utilisation has remained below its long-term average in domestic-oriented industries but has reached historical highs in export-oriented sectors (Figure 2, second panel).

The following paragraphs discuss in more detail the forces shaping the recovery. The chapter then goes on to examine how economic activity has been reflected in the labour market, price performance and the external balance. It concludes with an assessment of the short-term outlook. The policy setting impacting on recent and future economic performance is reviewed in the following two chapters of the Survey.

Strong export performance

The prominent role of export volumes in supporting the economic upturn is illustrated by the fact that, since the end of the 1990-91 recession, their share of real GDP has increased from 30 to 38 per cent. In 1994, exports rose by more than 14 per cent in volume, thereby contributing almost 5 percentage points to GDP growth. The pick-up in export growth can be attributed both to robust demand in the United States (which account for the bulk of Canadian exports) and a substantial improvement in competitiveness (owing to both a lower Canadian dollar and a fall in unit labour costs) as well as the influence of the Canada/US Free Trade Agreement (which came into effect in 1989). The increase in merchandise exports in 1994 was led by machinery and equipment, but most other major export categories (including automobiles and commodities) experienced double-digit growth rates. Since the beginning of 1995, export demand has weakened markedly (Table 1) as automobile sales in the United States tumbled.

Sustained business investment

Business fixed investment has been the second pillar of the recovery, growing by almost 10 per cent in 1994 as a rebound in non-residential construction added to the continued strength of machinery and equipment investment

Table 1. Demand and output

Volume percentage change, annual rates

	1979/ 1973	1989/ 1979	1994/ 1989	1992	1993	1994	Q1 1995/ Q4 1994	Q2 1995/ Q1 1994
Private consumption	4.4	3.1	1.0	1.3	1.6	3.0	0.1	0.9
Government consumption	3.5	2.5	1.1	1.0	0.5	–1.7	0.9	–0.8
Gross fixed investment	5.1	5.3	–0.1	–1.5	0.6	7.2	–1.8	0.3
Public	–0.3	3.8	3.6	–0.1	0.7	5.7	1.2	–10.7
Private	5.9	5.5	–0.6	–1.7	0.5	7.5	–2.3	2.1
Residential	3.4	4.5	–3.4	7.9	–4.2	3.0	–16.1	–15.2
Non residential	7.8	6.0	0.7	–5.5	2.7	9.4	3.2	8.8
Final domestic demand	**4.3**	**3.5**	**0.8**	**0.6**	**1.1**	**2.9**	**–0.2**	**0.4**
Stockbuilding [1]	0.1	–0.1	0	–0.2	0.9	0.3	3.5	0.3
Total domestic demand	**4.4**	**3.4**	**0.8**	**0.4**	**2.0**	**3.2**	**3.3**	**0.8**
Exports of goods and services	4.6	5.2	7.5	7.6	10.4	14.2	4.6	–13.0
Imports of goods and services	6.0	6.4	6.0	5.6	8.8	10.5	10.2	–7.3
Foreign balance [1]	**–0.2**	**–0.4**	**0.4**	**0.5**	**0.3**	**1.1**	**–2.1**	**–2.5**
Error of estimate [1]	0.1	0	0	–0.1	–0.1	0.2	–0.2	0.7
GDP at market prices	**4.2**	**3.1**	**1.1**	**0.8**	**2.2**	**4.6**	**0.9**	**–1.0**
of which:								
Agriculture	–0.2	2.3	0.8	–5.0	6.7	3.9	–3.3	–7.5
Mining	–4.1	1.0	2.9	2.1	5.0	6.3	2.4	–0.8
Manufacturing	2.5	2.1	0.3	1.3	4.8	7.0	3.9	–5.9
Construction	4.5	3.4	–2.0	–5.5	–2.0	5.4	–8.3	–13.2
Services	4.8	3.4	1.4	1.1	2.2	3.2	0.1	1.7

1. Contribution to GDP volume growth.
Source: Statistics Canada, National Income and Expenditure Accounts.

(Figure 3). Capital spending has been boosted by high capacity utilisation in export-oriented industries where it increased by 23¹/₂ per cent in 1994. Investment growth was highest in resource-based sectors such as primary metals, rubber, wood, paper and mining. More recently, the resurgence in corporate profits to pre-recession levels has also supported capital spending. In contrast to consumer sentiment, business confidence has remained relatively high. The mid-year survey of Public and Private Investment Intentions showed an upward revision to expected spending levels in 1995, despite the slowing in overall demand growth.

In addition to the above influences which have gained importance more recently, machinery and equipment investment has continued to be underpinned by "input restructuring", that is a shift towards greater use of capital relative to

Figure 3. **BUSINESS FIXED INVESTMENT**

Year-on-year volume change

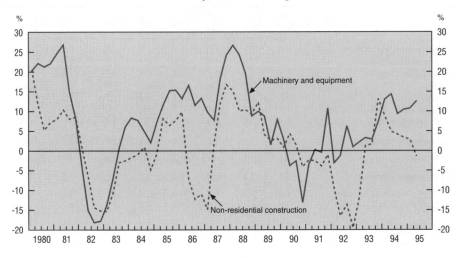

Source: CANSIM – Statistics Canada.

labour in the production process in response to relative price changes. The sharp decline in the cost of computer-based technology (by about one-half since the late 1980s) has provided much of the impetus for firms to restructure. Over the past five years, the proportion of computer purchases in total expenditure on machinery and equipment has increased from 18 to 37 per cent in volume terms. Another factor leading firms to employ relatively more capital was the emergence of a wide gap between the real cost of labour and the level of labour productivity in the 1990s. Such a ''producer real wage gap'' (that is, the difference between the real wage measured in terms of producer prices at factor costs and real output per worker) can be expected to appear during a cyclical downswing, as productivity growth slows while wages adjust only with a lag. But usually (as, *e.g.* in the early 1980s, see Figure 4) it is short-lived. Its size and relatively long persistence in recent years reflects substantial increases in payroll taxes, as discussed in Chapter III, as well as a slow adjustment of wage increases to the sudden decline of inflation to rates not seen since the early 1960s.

8

Figure 4. THE "REAL WAGE GAP"

Seasonally adusted

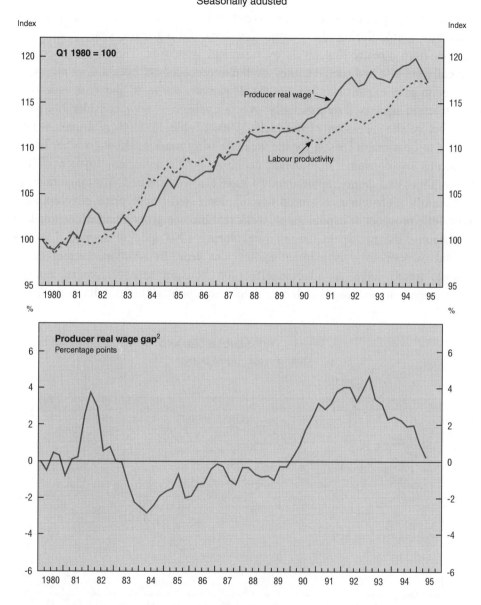

1. Labour income, per head, divided by the GDP deflator.
2. Difference between producer real wage and labour productivity.
Source: OECD, *National Accounts.*

Weak household demand

In stark contrast to business investment, residential investment has been unusually weak during the current recovery, falling back sharply in recent months from already low levels by historical standards. The housing sector is typically volatile and such declines are not unprecedented, both during recessions and economic expansions (Figure 5). However, while in the past residential construction increased substantially over a cycle, it is now considerably lower than before the recession of the early 1990s (Table 1). High real interest rates appear to be a major reason for the weak housing market, although other factors – such as low consumer confidence, declining public sector employment, falling house prices and demographic trends – have also contributed. Mortgage rates are particularly high when measured against depressed house price developments. With little prospect of capital gains, weak real income growth and widespread job uncertainty, the run-up in interest rates during 1994 quickly aborted a modest revival in residential investment earlier that year. In addition, current demographic trends have an adverse effect on housing activity: annual housing requirements are estimated to have fallen from about 190 000 units in the 1980s

Figure 5. **HOUSEHOLD DEMAND**
Year-on-year volume change

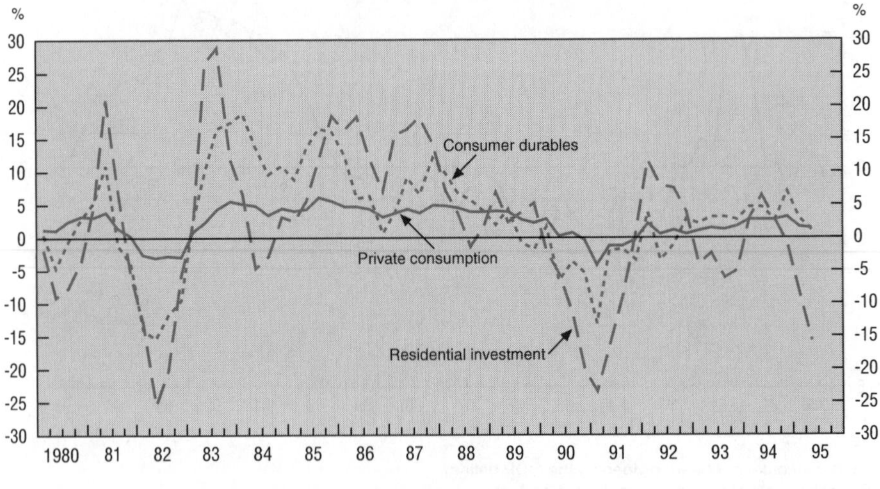

Source: CANSIM – Statistics Canada.

10

to about 150 000 units in 1994.[1] Still, housing starts have dropped far below this level in recent months. However, sales of existing housing have started to recover.

While contributing to the recovery, private consumption has proved much less supportive than in the past (Figure 5, Table 1). This reflected relatively modest demand for durables, which normally are the driving force behind cyclical rebounds of consumer spending in Canada. The major factors underlying this trend are weak real disposable income growth, a high level of personal indebtedness, low consumer confidence and relatively high real interest rates. In 1994, however, there were signs of a strengthening of consumer demand following a fall in real long-term interest rates and steepening of the yield curve, which had a positive short-term substitution effect on consumer spending. But these developments were reversed subsequently, prompting a marked decline in purchases of consumer durables in early 1995. Private consumption would have been even weaker if the household saving ratio had not dropped significantly in 1994, following four years of relative stability. This has been in part explained by the fast growth in household assets – in particular stock market assets, insurance and pension funds – which has led to growth of household net worth in excess of the rise in disposable income, despite continued increases in personal debt. It is also worth noting that while the measured personal saving ratio is now quite low by historical standards, it is not when adjusted to remove the effect of lower inflation in the 1990s. Hence, there is little reason to expect a strong rebound in the measured saving ratio beyond the increase that occurred in early 1995 in response to higher interest rates.

Persistent labour-market slack

After fluctuating in the 11 per cent range during the first three years of the recovery, the unemployment rate fell markedly during 1994 but has stabilised at around 9½ per cent since (Table 2). This mirrored the trend of employment, which, after some pick-up during 1994, has risen little. Such a development masks, however, two divergent developments: public-sector employment has fallen by more than 200 000 since November 1994 and this has been more than offset by a continued increase in private-sector employment. Despite its fall from cyclical peaks, unemployment has stayed well above its "natural rate", which is

Table 2. **Labour supply and demand**

Percentage change, annual rates

	1979/ 1973	1989/ 1979	1994/ 1989	1992	1993	1994	August 1995/ August 1994
Working age population	2.2	1.4	1.6	1.7	1.7	1.5	1.3
Labour force	3.2	2.0	0.9	0.5	1.3	1.1	0.4
Employment	2.9	2.0	0.3	–0.6	1.4	2.1	1.2
Goods producing sector	1.6	0.5	–2.1	–4.1	0	2.9	2.7
Service sector	3.6	2.6	1.2	0.7	1.8	1.8	0.7
	1974-79	1980-89	1990-94	1992	1993	1994	August 1995
Unemployment rate[1]	7.2	9.4	10.3	11.3	11.2	10.4	9.6
Participation rate[2]	61.7	65.8	66.1	65.9	65.6	65.3	64.8
Employment ratio[2]	57.3	59.7	59.3	58.4	58.2	58.5	58.6
	1979/ 1973	1989/ 1979	1994/ 1989	1992	1993	1994	
Memorandum items:							
Labour productivity	1.3	1.1	0.8	1.3	0.8	2.4	
Total factor productivity[3]	0.8	0.5	–0.3	0.1	0.7	2.6	

1. Per cent of labour force.
2. Per cent of population 15 years and over.
3. Business sector.
Source: Statistics Canada.

estimated to have declined from over 9 per cent to around 8½ per cent over the past two years or so in response to labour market reforms. Moreover, the improvement in the labour market has been less pronounced than it first appears, given that employment has increased only slightly faster than the working-age population while labour-force participation has continued to fall. Had the participation rate returned to its pre-recession level, as it did in the cycle of the early 1980s (Figure 6), the unemployment rate would now be around 2½ percentage points higher.

The fact that the labour-force participation rate has not rebounded is puzzling, given that, for the first time in the current cycle, 1994 has seen a shift from part-time to full-time employment. The major reason appears to be that, in stark contrast to the upturn in the 1980s, the ratio of employment to working-age population – an overall indicator of job opportunities – has hardly risen so far (Figure 6). Employment prospects for the unskilled have been particularly dismal, leading to the largest declines in participation being found among the least

12

Figure 6.   **LABOUR FORCE, EMPLOYMENT AND UNEMPLOYMENT**

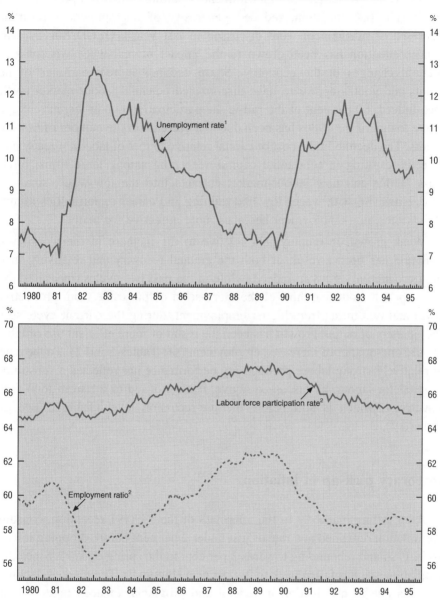

1.   Per cent of labour force.
2.   Per cent of working age population.
Source: CANSIM – Statistics Canada.

13

educated youth. A number of other influences putting downward pressure on the participation rate (taxation, reduced generosity of unemployment insurance, higher school attendance) were discussed in last year's OECD Survey. More recently, attention has been drawn to the impact of real wage weakness and structural changes in the economy. Sharp declines in real earnings of new entrants and youths appear to have discouraged potential labour-market partici- pants. Indeed, 80 per cent of the fall in the participation rate in the current cycle relative to that of the 1980s has been due to a decrease in the number of first-time entrants. The decline in the cost of capital relative to that of labour, already noted above, is resulting in substantial capital deepening among large firms, forcing excess labour and new labour-market entrants into the low-wage, small-firm sector. However, with wages low and training and career opportunities minimal in this sector, non-employment becomes more attractive for many.

Weak growth in employment relative to the increase in the working-age population has been a result of both the gradual recovery and relatively strong labour productivity growth. Indeed, while in the past two cycles (measured from peak to peak) about one-third of the increase in output came from productivity growth and two-thirds from higher employment, during the current cycle so far three-quarters of output growth has been the result of more efficient use of labour and only one-quarter of increased employment (see Tables 1 and 2). To the extent that relatively strong labour productivity performance has reflected a substitution of capital for labour, as discussed above, it has not led to a rise in total factor productivity, which is still below the pre-recession level (Table 2; see also Chapter IV).

Temporary pick-up in inflation

After falling markedly in the aftermath of the 1990/91 recession, consumer price inflation remained at a rate of just under 2 per cent before dropping towards zero in 1994 and rebounding towards 3 per cent in the spring of 1995. Since then, the inflation rate has fallen back to 2¼ per cent (Figure 7). The marked decline in 1994 was due to a reduction in federal and provincial tobacco taxes (to curb smuggling across the border with United States) which lowered the level of the consumer price index (CPI) by 1.3 per cent. Abstracting from this factor, inflation was broadly stable from early 1993 to early 1995. The subsequent pick-up in the

Figure 7. **INFLATION INDICATORS**
Percentage change over 12 months

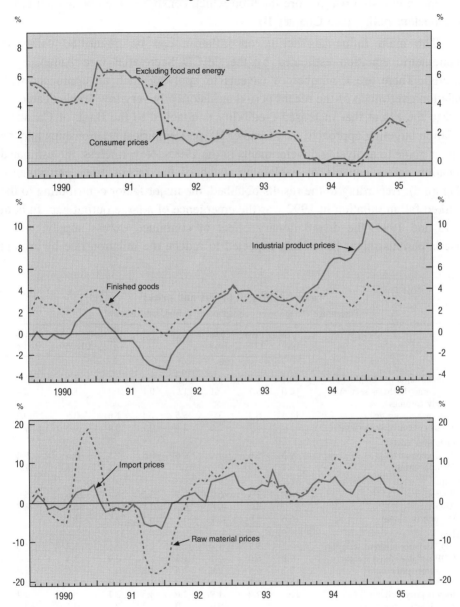

Source: CANSIM – Statistics Canada.

15

annual CPI increase reflected initially the disappearance of this special factor but subsequently also a rise in core inflation which constitutes the operational target of monetary policy (see Chapter II).

The main influences acting on inflation can be quantified using an econometric equation estimated by the OECD Secretariat (see Annex I for details). There are a number of caveats to applying such an approach: with inflation over much of the recent period at historically very low levels (Table 3), and to the extent that increased credibility is attached to the Bank of Canada's inflation targeting approach[2] (see Chapter II), past empirical relationships may be a poor guide to analysing developments in the 1990s. Nevertheless, the estimated equation seems capable of explaining much of the recent price performance (Figure 8). According to the results obtained, the major factor contributing to the marked fall in inflation in 1992 was the emergence of a large output gap. In both 1993 and 1994, the disinflationary effect of continued excess supply, which ceteris paribus might have been expected to reduce the inflation rate by around

Table 3. **Wages, profits and prices**

Percentage change over corresponding period, annual rates

	1979/ 1973	1989/ 1979	1994/ 1989	1992	1993	1994	Q1 1995/ Q1 1994	Q2 1995/ Q2 1994
Wages								
Compensation per employee	10.7	6.6	3.1	3.2	1.0	1.2	1.3	0.4
Wage rate (business sector)	10.0	6.7	2.1	1.9	0.1	1.8	1.5	0.4
Hourly earnings in manufacturing	11.6	6.3	3.3	3.5	2.1	1.6	0.5	0.9
Major collective settlements		6.7	2.6	2.4	0.7	0.4	0.8	1.0
Unit labour costs								
Total economy	9.3	5.6	1.9	1.6	–0.5	–1.5	–0.3	0.4
Manufacturing	9.4	4.9	0.2	–1.2	–2.5	–1.8	–4.3	–1.7
Profits								
Pre-tax	14.8	5.3	–0.9	0.7	20.2	36.1	28.6	15.0
After-tax	15.2	4.0	–0.8	4.3	64.4	51.8	36.2	18.9
Per unit of output	10.6	1.9	–2.1	–0.1	16.5	29.1	21.9	
Prices								
GDP deflator (current weights)	9.2	5.7	1.8	1.2	1.0	0.6	1.3	1.9
GDP deflator (fixed weights)	9.8	6.0	2.1	1.3	1.5	0.9	2.4	2.8
Consumer price index	9.2	6.5	2.8	1.5	1.8	0.2	1.6	2.7
Private consumption deflator	8.6	6.1	2.6	1.3	1.7	0.7	1.3	1.8
Import price deflator	10.7	2.0	1.9	2.6	4.3	3.7	5.2	2.4
New housing price index			–0.9	0	1.2	0.1	–0.4	–0.9

Source: Statistics Canada; OECD, *National Accounts.*

16

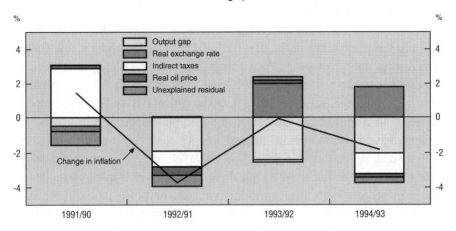

Figure 8. **EXPLAINING THE CHANGES
IN CONSUMER PRICE INFLATION**
Percentage points

Note: See Annex I for detailed explanations.
Source: OECD, Secretariat estimates.

2 per cent each year, was largely offset by the inflationary effect of the depreciation of the Canadian dollar. In fact, even taking account of the impact of indirect
tax changes, inflation in 1994 was slightly lower than would have been expected,
apparently reflecting a weak response of prices to exchange-rate depreciation.

Information presented in the Bank of Canada's May 1995 *Monetary Policy
Report* suggests that, at least for some sectors of the economy, exchange-rate
pass-through was slower than normal up to 1994. The clearest example of a full
exchange-rate effect was the motor vehicle sector. However, prices of a number
of other imported, or import-competing, consumer goods only partially reflected
the depreciation of the Canadian dollar, probably because of increased competition in many retail sectors due, in part, to the entry of big chains from the United
States. More recently, despite continued downward pressure on prices from the
output gap, lagged effects of the past decline in the Canadian dollar – the pass-
through is normally occurring over four quarters – have contributed to the
temporary pick-up in CPI inflation. In addition, there was a sharp increase in
world commodity prices over the past year, which was reflected in a marked rise
in industrial producer prices (Figure 7). Although driven by increases in prices of
export goods, these developments represent a significant rise in costs for domes-

tic producers. Nevertheless, the annual increase in producer prices of finished goods has remained relatively modest and has already started to decline in line with commodity prices (Figure 7).

Further declines in consumer price inflation will in part depend on the wage response to the price hikes in the first half of 1995. So far, there a few signs that wage pressures are developing. Notwithstanding some acceleration, overall wage increases have remained in the 1 to 2 per cent range (Table 3). New wage settlements, an indication of future wage developments, have also continued to be moderate, with a number of rollbacks in some industries. While private sector settlements have trended upward toward 1½ per cent, those in the public sector have remained at around ½ per cent as all levels of government are adopting positions of fiscal restraint. Although there are some examples of higher wage increases in sectors with strong productivity and/or profit gains, there is little evidence to suggest that stronger wage growth in booming export-oriented industries could spill over into other sectors of the economy. This is not surprising, given the weak demand conditions in domestic-oriented industries. The combination of rising productivity and moderate wage growth has led to declines in unit labour costs economy-wide in both 1993 and 1994 (and for the last three years in manufacturing). Although the recent economic slowdown and associated weakening of productivity growth has interrupted this process, unit labour costs were still only little higher than a year earlier by the second quarter of 1995 (Table 3).

Narrowing external deficit

The deficit on the external current account, which had remained stubbornly high since the late 1980s (Figure 9), has narrowed markedly recently, falling from 4 per cent of GDP in 1993 to below 3 per cent in the first half of 1995 (Table 4). While helped by a significant decline in the travel deficit, this improvement mainly reflects the strong rise in the merchandise trade surplus associated with booming export demand up to late 1994. Nonetheless, in relation to GDP, the trade surplus is still much smaller than in the early 1980s. This reflects the fact that recent gains in real export market share have only to a small extent reversed previous market losses, while import penetration has been rising steadily (Figure 9). In addition, Canada's terms of trade are slightly less favourable than at the beginning of the 1980s.

Figure 9. **THE CURRENT BALANCE AND ITS MAJOR COMPONENTS**

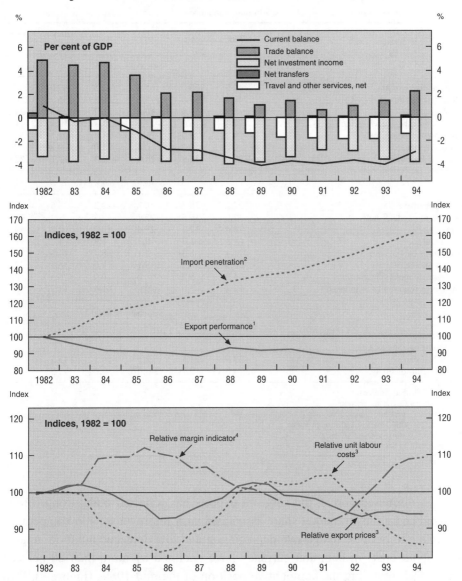

1. Cumulative export market gains (losses) for manufactures (in volume terms).
2. Ratio of imports to domestic demand plus exports (in volume terms).
3. In manufacturing. Common currency.
4. Ratio of relative export prices to relative unit labour costs.
Source: CANSIM – Statistics Canada; OECD, *National Accounts,* Secretariat estimates.

19

Table 4. **Balance of payments**[1]

C$ billion, annualised

	1991	1992	1993	1994	1995 Q1	1995 Q2
			Seasonally-adjusted			
Merchandise exports	144.5	159.8	185.8	223.5	259.0	251.8
Merchandise imports	140.1	152.8	175.6	206.8	235.7	230.3
Trade balance	**4.4**	**7.0**	**10.2**	**16.7**	**23.3**	**21.5**
Travel and other services, net	−12.4	−13.0	−13.4	−11.1	−10.4	−11.4
Investment income, net	−19.2	−20.0	−26.1	−28.9	−32.7	−32.6
Transfers, net	0.1	0.2	0.4	1.0	0.8	0.5
Current balance	**−27.0**	**−25.8**	**−28.8**	**−22.3**	**−19.1**	**−22.0**
			Not seasonally-adjusted			
Current balance	−27.1	−25.7	−28.7	−22.2	−28.5	−22.8
Long-term capital,[2] net	12.9	10.4	25.1	12.3	−1.4	41.7
Private	14.6	12.1	25.4	14.2	−0.2	43.2
Official[3]	−1.8	−1.7	−0.3	−1.9	−1.2	−1.5
Short-term capital, net	11.4	8.3	3.1	8.4	41.6	−18.2
Non-monetary[4]	6.5	14.2	3.1	7.5	16.1	22.3
Private monetary institutions	4.9	−5.9	0	0.9	25.5	−40.5
Change in reserves (+ = increase)	−2.8	−7.0	−0.6	−1.6	11.7	0.7
			Seasonally-adjusted			
Memorandum items:						
Current balance (s.a.)						
US dollars	−23.6	−21.4	−22.3	−16.3	−13.5	−16.1
Per cent of GDP	−4.0	−3.7	−4.0	−3.0	−2.5	−2.8

1. OECD/IMF definitions.
2. Excludes special transactions.
3. Including portfolio transactions of public authorities and Canadian Government utilisation of revolving standby credit facilities with domestic and foreign banks.
4. Including errors and omissions.
Source: OECD Secretariat.

As discussed above, the surge in exports has reflected both strong foreign demand and gains in market share associated with improvements in competitiveness. Due to both exchange-rate depreciation and low domestic inflation, relative unit labour costs in common currency have declined by more than 20 per cent since 1991, restoring the competitive position of the mid-1980s (Figure 9). With relative export prices falling somewhat less, the export sector's profitability has strongly improved. However, although Canadian suppliers' competitive position has also improved in domestic markets, the import propensity has remained high. In 1994, import volumes grew by more than 10 per cent overall, and by around

15 per cent for merchandise goods. This has limited the improvement in the trade balance, despite some rise in the terms of trade. In part, the strength of imports can be traced to the composition of demand in recent years, with both exports (especially automobiles) and machinery and equipment investment having a high import content. The growth of intra-industry trade, particularly in the automotive sector, which has been enhanced by the free trade agreements with the United States and Mexico, is an important factor explaining the close relationship between export and import developments (see also Chapter IV).

Canada's invisibles deficit, which was roughly stable from the late 1980s to the early 1990s, has widened markedly in recent years. This is attributable to diverging developments in the service and investment income accounts. The rise and subsequent fall of the Canadian dollar led to a temporary increase in the travel deficit which has been largely reversed since (Figure 9). Lower profit payments abroad by foreign firms based in Canada damped the investment income deficit in the early 1990s, but with improved profit performance more recently dividend payments outside the country have increased markedly. Underlying the trend in the investment income deficit, however, has been the steady rise in debt servicing costs, with the net interest payments abroad approaching 4 per cent of GDP. At the present level of the current account deficit, the conditions are in place for the external debt-to-GDP ratio to stabilise, provided that interest rates continue to decline (see the fiscal policy section in Chapter II).

Short-term outlook

Latest indicators suggest that economic activity remained weak until mid-1995 (Figure 10), and an inventory correction is likely to have limited production growth more recently. Following this growth pause, however, real GDP is projected to pick up from late 1995 and through 1996 (Table 5), growing again above the estimated rate of expansion of productive capacity. This growth profile reflects a renewed stimulus from demand in the United States and an increasingly positive impact of recent and expected monetary easing on economic activity. With buoyant corporate profits and rising capacity utilisation, business investment should remain relatively strong. The past rise in mortgage rates may continue to curtail housing demand in the near term, before increasing demographic requirements (see above) and improving housing affordability (due

21

Figure 10. **SHORT TERM ECONOMIC INDICATORS**

3 month moving average, change over 12 months

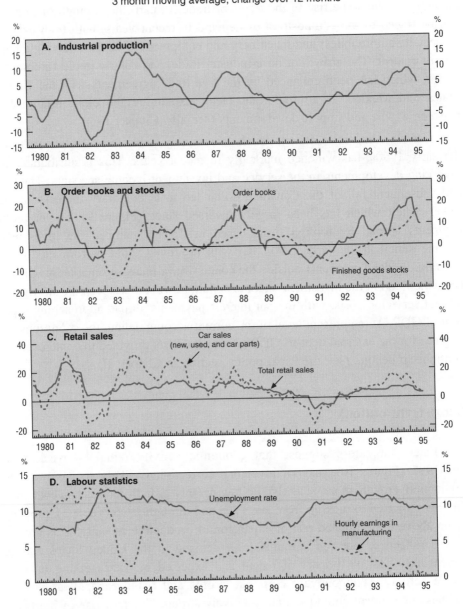

1. Includes mining and utilities.
Source: CANSIM – Statistics Canada.

Table 5. **Short-term projections**

Percentage changes, seasonally-adjusted annual rates, volume (1986 prices)

	1991 C$ billion[1]	1995	1996	1995 I	1995 II	1996 I	1996 II
Private consumption	412.0	1.7	2.9	1.2	2.0	2.9	3.6
Government consumption	144.9	-0.4	-0.3	-0.1	-0.3	-0.5	0.1
Gross fixed investment	132.0	2.9	5.8	1.1	4.7	6.0	6.5
Public[2]	16.4	5.8	4.5	2.7	5.0	5.0	3.0
Private residential	39.9	-9.8	3.4	-14.8	0.4	3.5	6.2
Private non-residential	75.6	7.3	6.9	7.2	6.2	7.0	7.3
Final domestic demand	**688.8**	**1.5**	**2.9**	**0.9**	**2.2**	**2.9**	**3.6**
Change in stockbuilding[3]	-3.2	0.3	-0.5	1.7	-1.8	-0.3	0.3
Total domestic demand	**685.6**	**1.9**	**2.3**	**2.7**	**0.3**	**2.6**	**3.9**
Exports of goods and services	164.8	10.9	7.8	5.5	7.7	7.8	7.9
Imports of goods and services	172.8	9.5	6.1	8.8	5.2	6.3	6.4
Change in foreign balance[3]	**-8.0**	**0.4**	**0.7**	**-1.3**	**1.0**	**0.6**	**0.6**
Statistical discrepancy[3]	-1.2	0	0	0	0	0	0
GDP at market prices	**676.5**	**2.3**	**3.1**	**1.3**	**1.3**	**3.2**	**4.5**
Inflation							
GDP implicit price deflator		2.0	2.0	2.2	2.4	2.0	1.8
Private consumption deflator		1.8	1.9	1.9	2.1	1.9	1.9
Industrial production		**5.0**	**4.2**	**2.7**	**2.6**	**3.8**	**4.7**
Unemployment rate[4]		**9.6**	**9.3**	**9.6**	**9.6**	**9.5**	**9.1**
Current balance (US$ billion)		**-14.2**	**-11.6**	**-14.8**	**-13.6**	**-12.2**	**-10.9**

1. Current prices.
2. Excluding nationalised industries and public corporations.
3. Contribution to GDP volume growth.
4. As a percentage of the labour force.
Source: OECD Secretariat.

to falling interest rates) lead to some revival next year. Consumer demand will also be supported by lower interest rates as well as renewed employment growth. In addition, substantial pent-up demand for automobiles and other durable goods should boost consumer spending. But the fact that the household saving ratio is already at a historically low level is likely to limit the scope for a significant strengthening of consumption growth.

The strong improvement in international competitiveness – assumed in the projections to be maintained – should allow Canadian exporters to continue to gain market share. Favourable export performance, together with projected more moderate import price increases, is expected to make for a further decline in the current account deficit. Despite employment growth, further inroads into unemployment are projected to be limited because labour-force participation should finally start rising. With continuing – though diminishing – slack in labour and product markets, inflation is expected to fall below the middle of the official target band of 1 to 3 per cent in 1996.

The above projections, which are based on information available in September 1995, embody the following assumptions:

- Reflecting strengthening growth in the United States, Canada's export markets are expected to expand at an annual rate of just under 8 per cent through 1996.
- The average OECD crude-oil import price is assumed to rise in line with OECD export prices for manufactures from $16 per barrel in the second half of 1995.
- Assuming constant exchange rates from September 1995, the rise in Canadian import prices is expected to slow to a rate of under 2 per cent in 1996.
- The cyclically-adjusted general-government financial balance is projected to improve by about 2 per cent of GDP over the two years to 1996.
- With interest-rate differentials *vis-à-vis* the United States narrowing, Canadian short and long-term rates are assumed to converge to 5¹/₂ and 7 per cent, respectively, in late 1996.

With sales to the United States now accounting for more than 80 per cent of total merchandise exports, growth prospects in Canada are strongly influenced by the conjuncture in its major trading partner. However, in view of considerable slack yet to be taken up and the favourable inflation prospects, the Canadian economy would seem to be in a position to achieve stronger growth than in the United States. Whether this can be realised will importantly depend on interest rate developments. Given the high level of Canada's public and external debt (see the next Chapter) and uncertainties about the future of the federation, financial-market nervousness may limit or delay the expected narrowing of interest-rate differentials *vis-à-vis* the United States, despite relatively favourable economic fundamentals.

II. Macroeconomic policies

With the recovery finally gaining momentum in 1994, the Canadian authorities have aimed at creating a healthy monetary and fiscal climate to establish the conditions for sustained economic growth and job creation. For monetary policy this has meant keeping consumer price inflation within a target band of 1 to 3 per cent, with a view to ensuring steadier economic expansion, a stable business climate, and lower interest rates. Fiscal policy has focused on halting and reversing the long-term deterioration in government finances with a view to achieving budget balance and to reducing public debt significantly relative to GDP.

The following paragraphs discuss macroeconomic policy developments in more detail. The conduct of monetary policy within the inflation-targeting framework is reviewed first, including some problems which may face policy-makers in the next few years. Fiscal policy and the budget outlook are then examined, with special emphasis on debt.

Monetary management

The current inflation-targeting framework

The objective of Canadian monetary policy is to promote good overall economic performance through price stability. Since 1991, the Bank has been committed to specific inflation-control targets along a path to price stability. The first set of targets – jointly announced by the government and the Bank – called for a gradual reduction in inflation to a range of 1 to 3 per cent by the end of 1995. In late 1993, the newly-elected government and the Bank agreed to extend the 1 to 3 per cent target through to end-1998 and to decide by 1998 on a target band that would represent an appropriate definition of long-term price stability. While the targets are set in terms of the annual increase in the total consumer price index (CPI), in its conduct of policy the Bank focuses on a core measure of the CPI which excludes the volatile food and energy components and the effects of changes in indirect taxes. As can be seen from Figure 11, after falling initially below the target band, core inflation tended to run close to the lower end of the target range during 1993 and 1994, before moving into the upper half of the range more recently. As discussed in Chapter I, this reflects the effects of past exchange-rate depreciation and higher commodity prices. The Government and the Bank expect core inflation, which has already eased to 2½ per cent, to move back towards the middle of the target range later in the year.

Because policy actions work slowly through the economy, taking effect over one or two years, projections and forward-looking indicators obviously play a crucial role in achieving the inflation targets. The Bank staff explicitly works out a projected path for the interest rate that is consistent with the desired inflation rate given the quarterly forecasts for other key variables, in particular the output gap and the exchange rate. At the same time, it monitors other possible indicators of future CPI inflation such as wage data, producer prices, and financial vari-

Figure 11. **INFLATION TARGETS**
Percentage change over 12 months

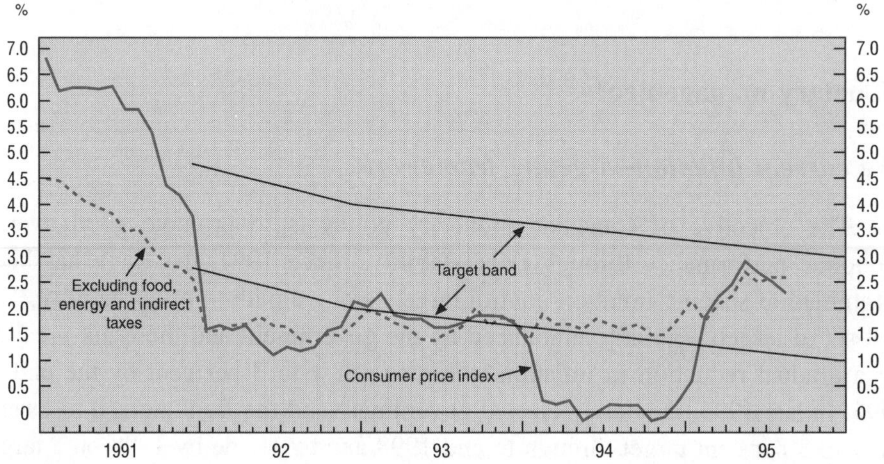

Source: CANSIM – Statistics Canada; Bank of Canada.

26

ables. Between formal forecasting exercises, the Bank uses a "monetary conditions index" (MCI) to capture the combined influence on the economy of short-term interest rates and the effective exchange rate. As these are the channels through which monetary actions are thought to have their principal effect, the MCI provides a shorthand measure of the overall degree of tightening or easing of policy. While the MCI serves as an operational target for monetary policy, the Bank must sometimes give precedence to steadying nervous markets. For this reason, and because the monetary conditions required to achieve the inflation-control targets is constantly reassessed as the economy is subject to shocks, the targeted range of the MCI is not published.

The Bank has, however, taken several initiatives to provide more transparency to its operations and reduce uncertainty about monetary policy. A semi-annual *Monetary Policy Report*, whose first issue appeared in May 1995, gives a detailed account of inflation developments and the conduct of monetary policy as well as a qualitative projection for inflation. Moreover, beginning in mid-1994, the Bank introduced a 50 basis points target range for the overnight loan rate. It announces changes in the target band without delay by offering deals to market participants at the new rates. The Bank thereby hopes to reduce the uncertainty about its intentions that has sometimes interfered with the transmission of policy actions to longer-term interest rates and the exchange rate. Finally, the authorities have decided to use foreign exchange market intervention as a "signalling tool", placing less emphasis on the moderation of exchange rate fluctuations. Intervention will be less frequent, but when it takes place, it will be carried out in a more visible manner with larger amounts.

Interest-rate and exchange-rate developments

In early 1994, short-term interest rates had dropped below 4 per cent, the lowest level for thirty years, and the exchange rate of the Canadian dollar had fallen back to the level prevailing in the mid-1980s (Figure 12). Throughout the spring, however, the dollar weakened and short-term interest rates rose sharply, with the net effect of some tightening in overall monetary conditions (as defined by the MCI). In part, this reflected external factors, notably the tightening of monetary policy in the United States. But interest-rate differentials between Canada and the United States also rose markedly (Figure 13), pointing to the influence of domestic developments (notably the budget situation and the forth-

27

Figure 12. **MONETARY CONDITIONS**

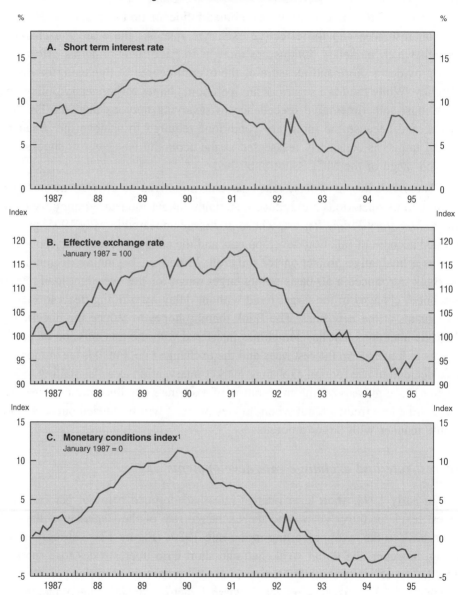

1. Index built by the Bank of Canada using a weighted average of changes in the interest rate and in the effective exchange rate.
Source: Bank of Canada.

Figure 13. **INTEREST RATE AND EXCHANGE RATE DEVELOPMENTS**

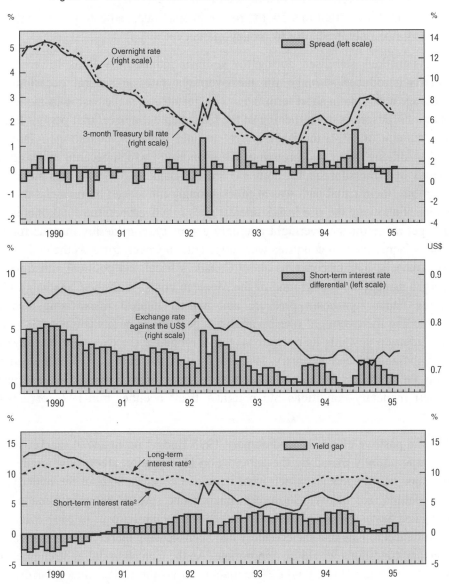

1. *Vis-à-vis* the United States.
2. 3-month corporate paper rate.
3. Over-10-year Government bond yield.
Source: CANSIM – Statistics Canada; OECD.

coming Quebec election). As can be seen from Figure 13, given the low inflation rate, the authorities tried to slow the rise in interest rates, adjusting the overnight financing rate only gradually to money-market rates.

As markets stabilised during the summer months, the Bank lowered the – newly-introduced – range for the overnight rate on several occasions to encourage a decline in short-term rates. This resulted in some easing in monetary conditions, despite a strengthening of the Canadian dollar over that period. In the early autumn of 1994, the Bank sought to hold monetary conditions relatively steady. Although the rapid growth of the economy – which became increasingly obvious over the subsequent months – led the Bank to desire tighter monetary conditions, their actual path was at times strongly influenced by financial-market factors. Following the rise in US interest rates in November, the Bank increased its target range for the overnight rate only gradually, considering that the fundamentals facing the two countries were different. However, towards the end of the year, financial-market concerns about Canada's fiscal and political situation re-emerged against the background of the Mexican crisis. With the Canadian dollar coming under significant pressure and market interest rates rising sharply – exceeding the overnight rate by almost 5 percentage points (Figure 13) – the Bank adjusted upwards its operational target range for the overnight rate several times in January and February 1995 to support the currency. This helped to steady the Canadian dollar, and thereby eased pressures on market interest rates, but left monetary conditions much tighter than in either mid-1994 or a year earlier.

The positive effect of the February 1995 Budget on financial market sentiment was initially muted by the anticipation of sovereign credit downgrades by the major rating agencies which have remained concerned about the underlying debt position (see below). Short-term interest rate spreads between Canada and the United States remained in the 2 per cent range until April. In May evidence began to accumulate that the economy had been slowing markedly and that easier monetary conditions would be appropriate. As the Canadian dollar strengthened, interest rates came down (and differentials *vis-à-vis* the United States narrowed). As a result, monetary conditions have eased significantly since their peak earlier in 1995. In contrast to mid-1994, however, the Bank did not have to encourage the interest rate decline, as evidenced by the negative spread between the market rates and the overnight financing rate (Figure 13). Given the Bank's monetary policy, the market saw such a decline as consistent with the slowing of economic activity.

Long-term interest rates have been less volatile. Broadly following trends in the United States, they have increased through 1994 and tended to fall since. With the sharp rise in short-term rates in early 1995, the yield curve – which was strongly upward sloping during the 1992-94 period – has flattened considerably (Figure 13). Notwithstanding some decline, long-term interest rates have remained significantly higher than abroad despite favourable inflation performance, with Canada/US spreads fluctuating in the 1 to 2 per cent range over the past eighteen months or so and staying in the upper end of that range recently. The persistent high risk premium on Canadian interest rates appears to reflect above all investor concerns about the rising public debt that might have translated into fears about long-term future inflation (see below).

Money and credit growth

The Bank views the monetary aggregate M2+ as a useful leading indicator of inflation pressures. Like most measures of broadly defined money, M2+ expanded unusually slowly in 1994 (Table 6). This reflected to a large extent a shift from deposits to mutual funds in the first half of 1994, which was later partly reversed as the relative rate of return on term deposits improved. Even allowing for these substitution effects, the growth of M2+ has been consistent with low inflation. The narrow aggregate M1 (deflated by a price index) provides information about future output levels. The high growth rate of this aggregate in 1994 conceals a sharp deceleration during the year associated with interest rate increases. Because of its volatility (which in part reflects special factors), real M1 has been difficult to interpret recently. But its recent pick-up suggests that the economy should continue to grow in the next few quarters.

Business credit expansion has strengthened over the past two years (Table 6) in line with investment spending, although higher profits have limited businesses' external financing needs. Though slowing, the increase in household credit has continued to exceed the growth of disposable income, causing the personal debt ratio to rise to a new high of around 90 per cent. Given depressed housing demand, the deceleration in mortgage credit has persisted. The growth of consumer credit, which was boosted by strong demand for durables in 1994, has slowed markedly since.

Table 6. **Money and credit**

Percentage change

| | 1991 | 1992 | 1993 | 1994 | Seasonally adjusted [1] | |
					1995 Q1	1995 Q2
Monetary growth						
Gross M1 [2]	2.5	5.9	9.1	12.1	7.9	7.8
M1 [3]	4.6	5.5	10.8	11.6	5.6	4.0
M2	6.8	3.7	3.2	2.3	4.5	4.5
M3	6.5	5.1	4.9	3.6	1.1	6.4
M2+	8.7	5.4	3.8	2.2	4.8	4.4
Credit expansion						
To business sector	3.5	2.0	0.5	4.3	5.4	5.2
of which:						
Short term	0.9	–3.3	–6.7	–0.2	9.7	5.0
To household sector	6.5	6.2	6.4	6.9	4.7	1.5
Consumer credit	2.1	–0.8	2.0	7.8	7.6	2.8
Residential mortgages	8.3	8.9	8.0	6.7	3.7	1.1
Memorandum items:						
Nominal GDP growth	1.0	2.0	3.3	5.2	3.5	1.9
Income velocity (GDP/M1)	–3.4	–3.3	–6.7	–5.8	–2.0	–2.0
Income velocity (GDP/M2)	–5.4	–1.6	0.1	2.9	–1.0	–2.5
Income velocity (GDP/M3)	–5.1	–2.9	–1.5	1.6	2.3	–4.3

1. Annual rate of change over preceding period.
2. Currency outside banks plus demand deposits.
3. Gross M1 minus private sector float, i.e. items in transit through the payment clearing system.
Source: Statistics Canada; OECD.

The challenges ahead

Although the current monetary policy framework appears to have contributed to the significant improvement in inflation performance in recent years, its robustness will only be fully tested as the recovery matures and economic activity approaches productive potential. Following the recent slowdown, this time may appear remote. However, the momentum of the upswing in 1994 had been generally underestimated by a wide margin. Given the crucial role inflation forecasts now play in guiding monetary policy decisions, the obvious difficulties in assessing and predicting the many forces that affect the economy and hence inflation are a potential problem for monetary policy.

In its first *Monetary Policy Report*, the Bank noted that, beyond the short term, the major concern is proper gauging of the speed and extent of closure in the output gap. The considerable uncertainty attached to this concept is illustrated by the fact that the size of the downward revisions of gap estimates in the early 1990s was larger than current estimates of the existing gap. OECD studies show that the extent to which the output gap exerts downward pressure on inflation depends not only on its size but also on how fast it is closed. However, calculations using a number of estimated empirical relationships (see Annex II) suggest that, even in the case of particularly high growth, this so called ''speed limit'' effect is not so large as to outweigh the disinflationary effect of a remaining output gap.

Instead, the main risk may not be a rapidly closing output gap *per se*, but rather that the momentum in the economy subsequently leads to an overshooting of potential. Research at both the Bank of Canada and the OECD[3] suggests that the resulting inflationary effects are stronger than the disinflationary impact of excess capacity. The importance of such ''asymmetric'' inflation consequences is illustrated by simulations using different versions of the OECD Secretariat's INTERLINK model (see Annex II). Several scenarios are examined, including ''hard landing'' variants where output initially overshoots potential and subsequently is reduced by restrictive policies by an amount equivalent to the overshoot in order to bring inflation back within the target range. The results are summarised in Figure 14. They show that, in the presence of asymmetric inflation effects, the consequences may be very costly in terms of output losses if inflation targets are to be met.

Another potential problem for monetary policy arises from the fact that, while the Bank has been right in stressing the potential benefits of Canada's hard-won status as a low inflation country, interest rates have not turned out to be as low, nor the Canadian dollar as firm, as might have been expected from the favourable inflation performance. The persistence of these developments could undermine confidence in the authorities' policy approach. It also complicates the operation of monetary policy and has adverse consequences for the economy. With a certain level of monetary conditions required to meet the inflation targets, high interest rates imply a lower exchange rate. Not that the resulting export-led growth has been unhelpful: it has led to a substantial narrowing in the external deficit and thereby reduced the use of foreign savings. But the high interest rates

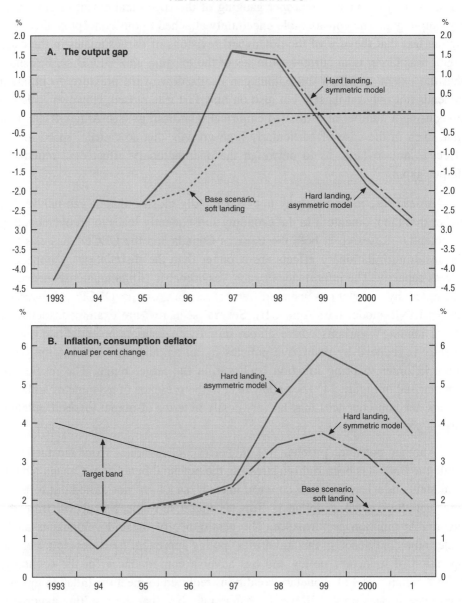

Figure 14. **THE OUTPUT GAP AND INFLATION:**
ALTERNATIVE SCENARIOS[1]

A. The output gap

Base scenario, soft landing

Hard landing, symmetric model

Hard landing, asymmetric model

B. Inflation, consumption deflator
Annual per cent change

Hard landing, asymmetric model

Hard landing, symmetric model

Target band

Base scenario, soft landing

1. For details, see Annex II.
Source: OECD, Secretariat simulations.

34

prevailing over the past year or so have constrained domestic demand from contributing much to recovery. Apart from restraining investment, they increase debt-service costs for all debtors, including governments. At the same time, they may encourage investments in the export-oriented sector that could prove misguided if the currency strengthens in the future.

As noted, a major factor behind the high risk premium in Canadian interest rates appears to be the high and rising level of public debt. Recent research by the OECD Secretariat[4] (Annex III) suggests that financial-market concerns about the risk to the value of investments reflect both inflation reputation (past inflation relative to that currently expected) and fiscal developments (on the belief that agents see them as a manifestation of inflation risk). It provides a possible explanation as to why Canada's favourable recent inflation performance has not translated into lower real long-term interest rates. The findings are summarised in Figure 15. They suggest that a long period of low and stable inflation has to be maintained before a sustained reduction in long-term rates follows, and that, in the case of Canada, the reduction in the interest rate premium that has occurred as

Figure 15. **CONTRIBUTIONS TO THE INFLATION RISK PREMIUM IN REAL LONG-TERM INTEREST RATES**

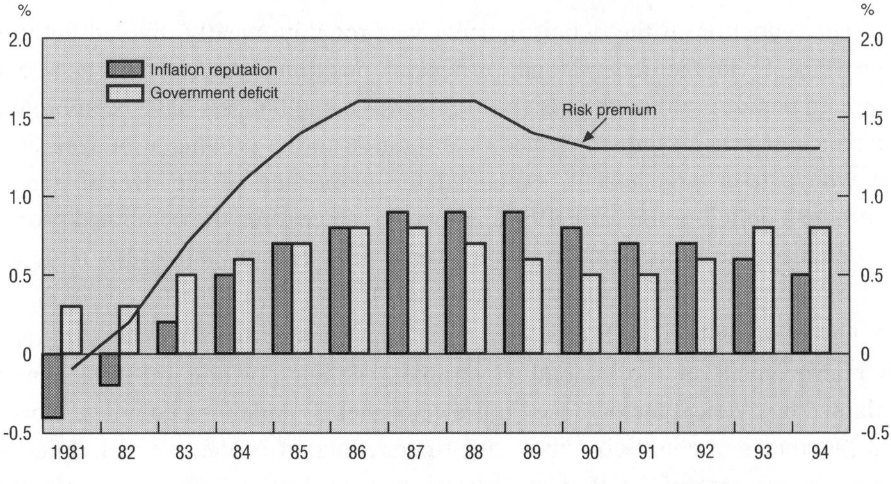

Source: OECD Secretariat estimates.

a result of improved inflation performance in the 1990s has been largely offset by the effect of higher budget deficits. It is true that, at the present time, fiscal and Quebec referendum effects appear to interact in raising doubts in investors' minds about the longer-run adherence to inflation targets. However, as discussed below, there is evidence that a reduction in government deficits would yield substantial economic benefits over the medium term.

Fiscal stance and budget outlook

General government

The strengthening of the recovery in 1994 was accompanied by a marked fall in the general government financial deficit, following five consecutive years of deterioration. On a national accounts basis,[5] the deficit declined by about 2 percentage points to 5.3 per cent of GDP in calendar year 1994. The OECD Secretariat is projecting a further fall in the deficit to below 4½ per cent of GDP in 1995 (see Figure 16). The improvement in 1994 has brought Canada more into line with the other major seven OECD countries: while in every year between 1982 and 1992 the deficit in Canada as a proportion of GDP was the second highest (behind Italy) amongst these countries, in 1994 it was back to a median position.

The reduction in the deficit in 1994 was roughly equally divided between improvements in the federal and provincial positions. As can be seen from Figure 16 panel A, although over the 1980s provincial budgets have been broadly in balance, it was an unprecedented deterioration in the provincial budget situation which, to a large extent, explained the worsening of the overall general government deficit in the early 1990s. However, since 1992 the combined provincial deficits have been on a downward trend. The federal deficit has remained more stable, but in the recent cycle peaked only in 1993.

Calculations by the OECD Secretariat suggest that just under two-thirds of the improvement in the general government deficit position in 1994 can be explained by cyclical factors (see Figure 16, Panel B) and that a complete closure of the output gap could contribute a further reduction in the cyclical deficit of about 1½ per cent of GDP. The Secretariat projection of a further substantial narrowing of the overall deficit in 1995 implies a discretionary fiscal tightening

Figure 16. **DECOMPOSITION OF THE GENERAL GOVERNMENT FINANCIAL BALANCE**
Per cent of GDP (National Accounts Basis)

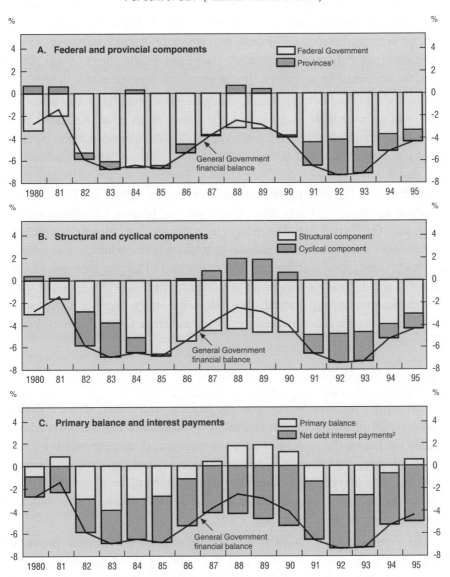

Note: 1995 data are OECD Secretariat projections.
1.   Including local government, hospitals, Canada and Quebec Pension Plans.
2.   Interest payments are shown with a negative sign.
Source: CANSIM – Statistics Canada; OECD, Secretariat estimates.

equivalent to nearly 1 per cent of GDP. This would still leave a structural deficit of just over 3 per cent of GDP, but the fact that a large part of the deficit is accounted for by net interest payments (see Figure 16, Panel C) suggests that the structural primary balance is already in substantial surplus. This provides an illustration of the burden which debt service places on the current fiscal position, despite the sustained improvement in the structural balance since 1993.[6]

Governments at both the federal and provincial level have announced their intention to balance their budgets over the medium term, as discussed further below. A common feature of fiscal consolidation plans has been their reliance on cutbacks in expenditure rather than increases in taxation.[7] The main reason for this is that relative to the United States the tax burden is already high and, despite the fact that taxation as a proportion of GDP is below the OECD average and well below the levels in many European countries, to most Canadians the comparison with the United States is most relevant given how closely integrated the two economies are. The recent increase in tobacco taxes, which led to a surge in cross-border smuggling and the subsequent reversal of the tax increase, is a good example of the difficulties which can be encountered if tax rates between the two countries become seriously misaligned. More generally, there is a concern that differences in tax burdens between them may influence firms' location decisions over the medium term.

Federal government

Following a more-or-less continuous year-on-year reduction in the deficit in the second half of the 1980s, the federal government was expecting to achieve a balanced budget by the mid-1990s. However, repeated slippage relative to fiscal plans in the early 1990s, mainly due to the deeper than expected recession, has meant that, despite recent improvement due to actions taken in the 1994 Budget, the likely deficit outcome for the financial year 1994/95 will be higher than it was at the beginning of the decade (see Table 7).

The February 1994 Budget, the first of the current Liberal government elected in October 1993, set out a plan for reducing the deficit that places the burden of adjustment on expenditure reduction. In contrast to previous years, the 1994 Budget did not include any medium-term fiscal projections beyond a two year horizon to 1995/96, although the new government was committed to reduce the deficit to an interim target of 3 per cent of GDP in 1996/97 on a public

Table 7. **Federal deficit: projections and outcomes**[1]

Public accounts basis; fiscal year (starting 1 April); per cent of GDP

	1990/91	1991/92	1992/93	1993/94	1994/95	1995/96	1996/97	1997/98
1990 Budget	4.5	4.4	3.2	2.1	1.2	0.7		
1991 Budget	4.2	3.7	2.7	1.7	1.1			
1992 Budget		4.6	3.8	2.9	1.7	1.0	0.6	
1993 Budget			5.2	4.5	3.8	2.5	1.6	0.9
1994 Budget				6.4	5.4	4.2	3.0	
1995 Budget					5.1	4.2	3.0	
Outcome	**4.8**	**5.1**	**6.0**	**5.9**	..	..	..	..

1. Figures along each row show the projected deficit (as a per cent of GDP) in a particular budget, except for the final row which gives the outcome for the deficit.
Source: Department of Finance.

accounts basis.[8] Measures to cut spending by the equivalent of about 1 per cent of GDP over two years included reductions in unemployment insurance benefits and in defence spending, as well as an extension of the civil service salary freeze. By contrast, the effects of revenue-raising initiatives were minimal, yielding under $1/4$ per cent of GDP, with measures to broaden the tax base largely offset by lower unemployment-insurance contributions and tobacco taxes.

According to recent estimates, the outcome for the federal deficit in 1994/95 is likely to under-shoot the 1994 Budget target by about C\$ 2 billion ($1/4$ per cent of GDP, see Table 8). Indeed, excluding the effect of special one-time restructuring charges relating to the costs of civil-service layoffs and the elimination of grain transportation subsidies (measures taken in the 1995 Budget, but accounted for in the financial year 1994/95), the under-shoot is estimated to have been nearly C\$ $4^1/2$ billion ($1/2$ per cent of GDP). The main reason for this is lower-than-expected programme spending of about C\$ 2 billion, primarily due to reduced expenditures on unemployment insurance benefits from better-than-expected labour market conditions. This, together with a C\$ $2^1/2$ billion unused contingency reserve and higher than expected non-tax revenues of C\$ 1 billion, more than offsets the effect of higher than anticipated interest rates on debt service of about C\$ 1 billion.

In the February 1995 Budget the government has maintained previous deficit targets, namely reducing the deficit to 4.2 per cent of GDP in 1995/96 (C\$ 32.7 billion) and 3 per cent of GDP in 1996/97 (C\$ 24.3 billion). Despite the

Table 8. **The 1994 and 1995 Federal Budgets**

Public accounts basis; fiscal year (starting 1 April); per cent of GDP

	1994 Budget	1995 Budget		
	Forecast 1994/95	Estimate 1994/95	Forecast 1995/96	Estimate 1996/97
Revenues	16.8	16.7	16.9	16.7
of which: Taxes	15.7	15.8	15.9	15.8
Expenditures	22.1	21.8[1]	20.8	19.3
of which:				
Programme spending	16.6	16.2[1]	14.5	13.1
Public debt charges	5.5	5.6	6.3	6.2
Deficit	**5.4**	**5.1**	**4.2**	**3.0**
Memorandum items:				
Net public debt	74.5	73.2	73.5	73.4
Deficit excluding public debt charges	−0.1	−0.5	−2.1	−3.2

1. Includes one-off restructuring charges equal to 0.35 per cent of GDP.
Source: Department of Finance.

likely under-shoot of the deficit in 1994/95, further action was required in the 1995 Budget to keep the deficit projections on track, given that higher-than-expected interest rates were expected to add the equivalent of almost 1 per cent of GDP to the deficit through increased debt service. The budget measures, once again, focused on spending cuts, these outweighing revenue increases by a ratio of 7 to 1. Thus, by 1996/97 programme spending (*i.e.* expenditure excluding debt service) is projected to have fallen by 12 per cent in real terms to its lowest share of GDP since 1950/51, whereas budgetary revenues as a proportion of GDP will remain roughly stable (see Figure 17).[9]

These deficit-cutting measures reflected a number of important initiatives by the Government. Firstly, more than half the fiscal savings in the 1995 Budget were the end result of a major ''Programme Review'' that closely considered which programmes and services the federal government should be providing, and the most effective and cost efficient way of doing so (see Chapter III for further details). The Budget also announced that the overall cost of the unemployment insurance programme would be eventually reduced by a minimum of 10 per cent, although the changes to the system that would bring about these savings will not

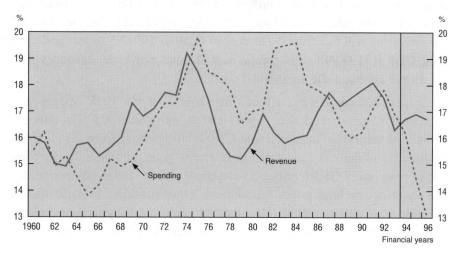

Figure 17. **FEDERAL BUDGETARY REVENUE AND PROGRAMME SPENDING**
Per cent of GDP

Note: 1994 to 1996 are projections from the 1995 Budget.
Source: Department of Finance.

be detailed until late 1995 (Chapter III includes some discussion of the likely form this will take).

Another significant budget initiative was the introduction of major changes in the system of transfers to the provinces with the aim of making them more cost effective and flexible. In addition to delivering spending cuts through reduced funding to provinces, these changes should lead to improved control of future federal spending (see Annex IV for details). Transfers under the Canada Assistance Plan (CAP), with funding of provincial social welfare programmes based on a shared-cost basis, will be merged with those under the Established Programs Financing (EPF) system, which provides block grants to finance provincial post-secondary education and health. This reform will be implemented in 1996/97, with the combined programme, the Canada Health and Social Transfer (CHST), made in the form of a block grant. Such a switch away from cost-sharing towards the provision of block grants should increase the incentive for provinces to limit additional social expenditure, which in the past has grown at an unsustainable rate, since individual provinces will bear the full incremental cost of any expan-

41

sion in their social welfare programmes, rather than being able to share it with the federal government. It will also provide the provinces with greater flexibility to allocate social expenditure to priority areas. As part of the reform total transfers to the provinces will fall from 5 per cent of GDP in 1994/95 to just under 4 per cent of GDP in 1997/98 (this compares with total provincial revenues of just under 19 per cent of GDP in 1994/95).

Business subsidies were a focus for savings in the 1995 Budget with a 60 per cent planned reduction, equivalent to more than C$ 2¼ billion, by 1997/98. The largest savings, of about C$ 0.6 billion, stem from the elimination of the subsidy to the rail transportation of prairie grain, although this involved a one-time payment of C$ 1.6 billion to owners of prairie land in compensation for the likely effect on land prices. In addition, other subsidies to agriculture and transportation as well as regional development, industry, the energy and resource sector and cultural industries all incurred across-the-board cuts (see also Chapter IV).

Other cuts in spending include a reduction in defence expenditure by about C$ 1.6 billion between 1994/95 and 1997/98 and a cut in overseas aid by C$ 0.5 billion over the same period. As a consequence of budget measures to cut or eliminate programmes there will be a reduction in federal employment of some 45 000 (about 15 per cent from 1994/95 levels) over three years, although some of these jobs will be transferred directly to the private sector as a result of privatisation (particularly in the transport sector).

On the tax side, the Budget included an increase in tobacco and gasoline excise duties and in corporate taxes. These measures, in addition to those designed to increase the fairness of the tax system and tighten loopholes, are expected to raise revenues by only C$ 1.4 billion (less than 0.2 per cent of GDP).

There are grounds to believe that the 1995 Budget targets for the deficit will be realised. Firstly, the economic assumptions on which the fiscal projections were based are relatively cautious, being more prudent than the average of private sector forecasts rather than representing ''best guess'' predictions. In particular, recent developments would suggest that average interest rates are likely to be almost 2 percentage points lower in 1995/96 than assumed in the Budget. This would even compensate for the effect on the deficit of a worst-case non-recessionary outcome for the real economy whereby real GDP remained flat throughout 1995/96.[10] In addition, the Budget incorporates contingency reserves of C$ 2.5 and C$ 3.0 billion in 1995/96 and 1996/97, which are not a source of funding for new policy initiatives, but rather are designed to cover the risks of unpredictable events and forecasting errors. A further reason for optimism regarding the deficit outcome is that a number of the spending cuts (especially to subsidies) and reforms implemented in the budget have reduced or eliminated expenditure in areas where the federal government's ability to exercise control has in the past been limited. Moreover, the new transfer system to the provinces, which – as indicated above – will mean the end of cost-sharing arrangements and their replacement by a single block transfer, should lead to a greater degree of control, albeit only from 1996/97. Nonetheless, federal government debt received a downgrading from one of the major credit-rating agencies (Moodys) following the 1995 Budget. This is less a reflection of the credibility of current plans for reducing the deficit than a recognition of the magnitude of the underlying fiscal problem in terms of the outstanding stock of government debt (see below).

Provincial governments

As noted above, the worsening in the provinces' fiscal position was the main factor behind the increase in the general government deficit in the early 1990s. In the three years to 1992/93 the combined provincial deficit, on a public accounts basis, rose from 0.7 to 3.6 per cent of GDP, more than double the increase in the federal deficit over the same period. The provincial deficit has since narrowed to 2.6 per cent of GDP in 1993/94 and to an estimated 2.0 per cent of GDP in 1994/95 (see Table 9).

The pressure towards achieving fiscal consolidation has been intensified by the reaction of financial markets, marked by downgradings of credit ratings during 1995. Indeed a clear relationship exists between provincial indebtedness, credit ratings and "interest rate spreads" (*i.e.* the difference between interest rates on provincial and federal bonds) faced by the different provinces (see Figure 18). Thus, provinces with higher net debt-to-GDP ratios tend to have lower credit ratings and higher interest rate spreads.[11] In many provinces the expected reaction of credit agencies has been an important consideration when drawing up budget plans.

As shown in Table 10, all of the provinces plan to eliminate their budget deficits with the exceptions of Quebec and Ontario, which envisage only balancing the current account (*i.e.* excluding capital spending) over the medium term. In

43

Table 9.   **Provincial deficits and debt**[2]

Public accounts basis; fiscal year (starting 1 April); percentage

	Proportion of total provincial expenditure	Ratio of deficit/surplus (+/−) to provincial GDP		Ratio of net debt to provincial GDP	Proportion of total provincial net debt
	1994/95	1994/95	1995/96	1994/95	1994/95
Ontario	34.9	2.7	1.8[3]	29.7	45.3
Quebec	27.4	3.4	2.3	33.6	27.9
British Columbia	12.8	0.4	−0.1	9.4	4.3
Alberta	9.4	−0.1	0.6	16.5	6.7
Manitoba	3.5	0.9	−0.2	29.2	3.2
Saskatchewan	3.3	−0.5	−0.1	32.8	3.5
Nova Scotia	3.1	1.6	0.9	43.6	3.7
New Brunswick	2.8	0.3	−0.4	36.8	2.6
Newfoundland	2.3	1.4	0.0	50.6	2.3
Prince Edward Island	0.5	0.4	−0.1	39.7	0.4
Total all provinces[1]	**100.0**	**2.0**[4]	**1.3**[4]	**27.1**[4]	**100.0**

1.   Provincial expenditure and net debt totals exclude the Territories.
2.   Figures for 1994/95 are estimated outcomes and figures for 1995/96 are based on the 1995 Budget projections.
3.   A new provincial government was elected in Ontario in June 1995, but the projected deficit for Ontario in 1995/96 is based on the 1995 Budget projections of the previous government, although the deficit projection of the new government is very similar.
4.   Total provincial deficit/debt as a proportion of national GDP.
Source: Department of Finance.

general, these fiscal consolidation plans are based on reducing expenditure, with action on the revenue side limited. Thus, in the 1995 Budgets there were no increases in personal or corporate income tax rates and even some tax reductions. Fulfilment of the 1995 Budget plans would imply a further reduction in the combined provincial deficit to about 1.3 per cent of GDP in 1995/96.

The main reason that progress will not be more rapid is that the two largest provinces, Ontario and Quebec, are lagging behind the fiscal consolidation efforts of the eight other provinces, which are all much closer to eliminating their deficits. Future provincial fiscal developments will thus depend heavily on the extent of fiscal consolidation in Ontario and Quebec: in 1994/95, these two provinces are estimated to account for about three-fifths of provincial expenditure, more than 70 per cent of outstanding provincial debt and nearly 95 per cent of the combined provincial deficit. In Ontario, a new provincial government was elected in June 1995 on a platform of balancing the budget, but only by the end

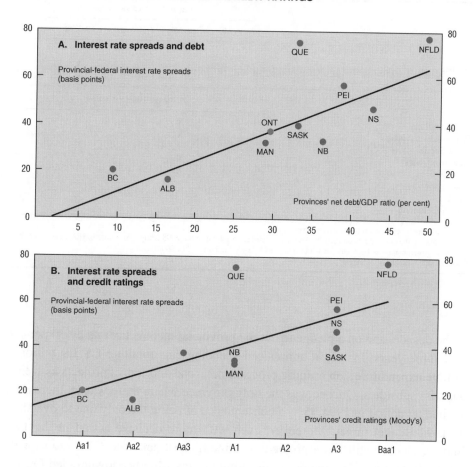

Figure 18. **PROVINCIAL INTEREST RATE SPREADS, DEBT AND CREDIT RATINGS**

Notes: ALB = Alberta; BC = British Columbia; MAN = Manitoba; NB = New Brunswick; ONT = Ontario; SASK = Saskatchewan; NS = Nova Scotia; PEI = Prince Edward Island; QUE = Quebec; NFLD = Newfoundland. The interest rate spread (variable "SPREAD") measures the difference, in basis points, between interest rates on provincial bonds and federal bonds in April 1995. The net debt-to-GDP ratio (variable "DEBT") are values for the financial year 1994/95. For the purpose of quantifying any relationship the variable "CREDIT" has been created and given the value of 1 for the highest provincial credit rating (Aa1), with successively lower credit ratings incremented by one. Estimated lines of best fit (with t-ratios in brackets) for all the provinces, excluding Quebec, are given by:

(1) SPREAD = 2.2 + 1.32 DEBT, R^2 = 0.792 ;
      (-0.2) (5.2)
(2) SPREAD = 5.4 + 7.95 CREDIT, R^2 = 0.766.
      (0.6) (4.8)

Source: Department of Finance and OECD Secretariat calculations.

Table 10. **Fiscal objectives in the 1995 provincial budgets**

	Target: balanced current account [1]				
	1994/95	1995/96	1996/97	1997/98	1998/99
Nova Scotia			X		
Quebec				X	
Ontario [2]				X	

	Target: balanced budget				
Newfoundland		X			
Prince Edward Island		X			
Nova Scotia			X		
New Brunswick		X			
Manitoba		X			
Saskatchewan	X				
Alberta			X		
British Columbia		X			

1. The current account excludes capital expenditures.
2. Balancing the current account in 1997/98 was the objective set out in the 1995 Budget for Ontario. However, since then a new government has been elected which plans to balance the budget in 2000/01.
Source: Department of Finance.

of the decade, and on a pledge to cut the provincial income tax rate by 30 per cent over three years. In July it announced spending cuts totalling C$ 1.9 billion in welfare expenditure, job training programmes, road and transit projects as well as business subsidies. Quebec was the only province where there was an increase in the budget deficit in 1994/95 as a consequence of being the only one to overshoot its 1994 Budget target. Moreover, even with more decisive action in the 1995 Budget, Quebec still has a projection of the highest deficit-to-GDP ratio for the current fiscal year. The major credit-rating agency Moodys downgraded Quebec in June 1995, citing failure to make sufficient progress in reducing the deficit despite three years of economic growth.

A further uncertainty concerns the reaction of the provinces to the reduction in transfers from the federal government which will take place in 1996/97 as part of the wider reform of the federal-provincial transfer system mentioned above. The widening of provincial deficits during the early 1990s, although mainly due to the unexpected severity of the recession, was exacerbated by federal government constraints on the growth of transfers to the provinces. However, several provinces have already announced that they would react to the reduction in transfers by either reducing expenditures and/or implementing revenue-raising measures in order to maintain their fiscal objectives. The adjustment problem could be made less difficult for provinces in the future if there was an early resolution to the contentious issue of how the new transfer payment will be allocated between them beyond 1996/97.

The debt constraint

With persistently high budget deficits, net general government debt in Canada has been rising steadily, from 13¹/₂ per cent of GDP in 1980 to over 64 per cent in 1994 (on a national accounts basis). Although similar trends are present in other major OECD economies, Canada's relative position has tended to worsen over time (see Figure 19): from having the second lowest net debt-to-GDP ratio amongst the major seven economies in 1980 to having the second highest (after Italy) in 1994. In the early 1980s the worsening debt position was a consequence of running large deficits on the primary balance (i.e. the total budget balance excluding interest payments, see Figure 16, Panel C). By contrast, since 1987 on average the primary balance has been only slightly in deficit, but interest payments to service the outstanding debt have averaged almost 5 per cent of GDP – about twice the average for the major seven economies.

The extent to which the level of government debt has a negative effect on the fiscal position depends critically on the difference between the interest rate and the growth rate.[12] Thus, assuming real GDP growing by 3 per cent (the OECD Secretariat's estimate of the growth rate of potential output over the medium term) and a real interest rate of 7 per cent (slightly below the average over the period 1990-94), a primary budget surplus equal to 2¹/₂ per cent of GDP is required merely to hold the net debt-to-GDP ratio constant at its 1994 level of 64 per cent (Table 11). Although this result is sensitive to the above assumptions, it gives some indication of the strain which the current debt burden places on fiscal policy, given that over the last twenty years a primary surplus of 2¹/₂ per cent of GDP has rarely been achieved even temporarily by any of the major OECD economies (with the exception of Japan). Furthermore, given the adverse effect of fiscal developments on economic performance, there is widespread recognition that the debt-to-GDP ratio needs to be reduced, rather than be held constant, over the medium term. The following discussion attempts to assess

Figure 19. **PUBLIC DEBT**[1]
As a percentage of GDP

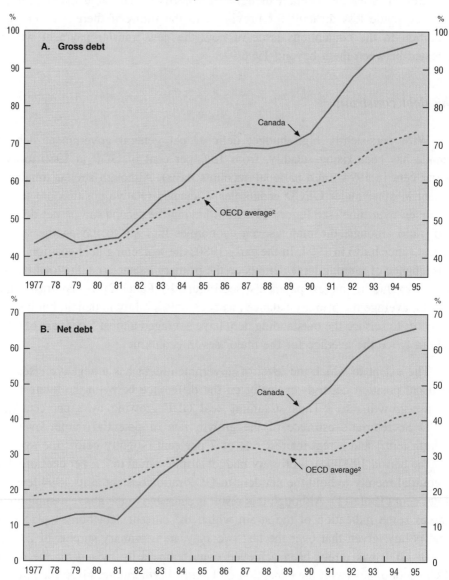

1. General government; national accounts definitions.
2. Weighted average of 17 countries (1987 GDP weights and exchange rates).
Source: OECD, *National Accounts*; Secretariat estimates.

Table 11. **Primary surpluses required to stabilise the net government debt-to-GDP ratio at the 1994 level**[1]

Per cent of GDP

Real interest rate (per cent)	Real growth rate (per cent, per annum)				
	2	2½	3	3½	4
9	4.5	4.2	3.9	3.6	3.2
8	3.9	3.6	3.2	2.9	2.6
7	3.2	2.9	2.6	2.3	1.9
6	2.6	2.3	1.9	1.6	1.3
5	1.9	1.6	1.3	1.0	0.6

1. Figures are calculated from the expression for the government's dynamic budget constraint (see Annex V).
Source: OECD Secretariat.

whether this is likely to be achieved on current policies, taking into account the interaction between macroeconomic performance and government finances.

As a result of the 1995 federal Budget, net debt will be some C$ 29 billion lower in 1996/97 (*i.e.* about 3 per cent of GDP) than it otherwise would have been. Nevertheless, even if the current fiscal targets are met at both the federal and provincial levels, the high net public debt-to-GDP ratio would only start falling gradually from 1996, and government finances would remain vulnerable both to a slowdown in the economy and changes in interest rates. This can be illustrated by simulations using the OECD Secretariat's INTERLINK model. As shown in Table 12, the baseline projection assumes that the government budget is brought into balance by the year 2001 by maintaining a substantial surplus on the primary balance. This is the result of virtually unchanged tax rates and real cutbacks in government expenditure in 1995 and 1996, followed by real current expenditure growth of only 1 per cent per annum thereafter, consistent with a fall in the ratio of government primary expenditure to GDP from 38 per cent in 1994 to 34 per cent in 2001. As a consequence, the net debt-to-GDP ratio would be reduced from 64½ per cent in 1994 to 54 per cent by 2001.

Such a scenario assumes that between 1995 and 2000 interest rates will fall by more than 2 percentage points. Every percentage point rise in interest rates (assuming it is at all maturities) above this assumption would "mechanically" add about 5½ percentage points to the debt ratio by 2001.[13] Thus, if interest rates did not decline at all from their 1995 levels, there could be no progress in

Table 12. **The sensitivity of medium-term fiscal projections
to macroeconomic performance**[1]

	1995	1996	1997	1998	1999	2000	2001
	Per cent						
Baseline projection							
GDP growth	2.3	3.1	4.2	3.5	3.2	3.1	3.1
Output gap	-2.4	-2.0	-0.7	-0.2	-0.0	-0.0	0.0
Short-term interest rates	7.2	5.7	5.2	5.0	4.8	4.6	4.5
Long-term interest rates	8.3	7.3	7.0	6.8	6.5	6.2	6.2
	Per cent of GDP						
Net primary balance	0.6	1.8	2.6	3.1	3.3	3.4	3.6
Net interest payments	5.0	4.9	4.6	4.4	4.0	3.7	3.7
Total budget balance	-4.4	-3.1	-2.0	-1.3	-0.7	-0.3	0.1
Net government debt	66.2	66.1	64.4	62.3	59.9	57.3	54.3
	Difference from baseline, per cent of GDP						
Effects of slower GDP growth[2]							
Net primary balance	-0.2	-0.4	-0.7	-0.9	-1.2	-1.4	-1.7
Net interest payments	0.2	0.4	0.2	0.4	0.5	0.6	0.7
Total budget balance	-0.4	-0.8	-0.9	-1.3	-1.7	-2.0	-2.4
Net government debt	0.6	1.7	2.8	4.2	6.0	8.0	10.3
Effects of higher interest rates[3]							
Net primary balance	0.0	0.0	0.0	0.0	0.0	0.0	0.0
Net interest payments	0.4	0.9	0.8	0.9	1.0	1.1	1.1
Total budget balance	-0.4	-0.9	-0.8	-0.9	-1.0	-1.1	-1.1
Net government debt	0.4	1.3	2.0	2.8	3.7	4.5	5.4

1. The simulations are carried out on the OECD Secretariat's INTERLINK macroeconomic model.
2. The simulation of lower growth involves lower GDP growth by $^1/_2$ per cent per annum, but with unchanged interest rates. In order to achieve this outcome, consumption is used to target the lower growth profile. Inflation is unchanged in the simulation because potential output is assumed to be reduced by a similar magnitude.
3. The simulation of higher interest rates involves an increase in interest rates at all maturities of 1 percentage point. For the purposes of this calculation the projection of the real economy is assumed to be unchanged.
Source: OECD Secretariat.

reducing the debt ratio, despite the assumed degree of fiscal restraint. In this respect, Government finances in Canada are more vulnerable to interest rate changes than in most other OECD economies.[14]

Fiscal developments are also sensitive to projections of the GDP growth rate. The baseline scenario projects growth averaging about $3^1/_4$ per cent per annum between 1995 and 2001, reflecting potential output of just under 3 per cent per annum with an output gap of about 2½ per cent in 1995 which is closed by 2001. A reduction in the average GDP growth rate by ½ per cent per annum would add 10 percentage points to the debt ratio by the year 2001, implying that there would be little overall reduction in government indebtedness relative to the position in 1994.[15] Again, similar exercises for other OECD economies suggest that Canada's debt position is one of the most vulnerable to the medium term macroeconomic outlook.

While the above calculations demonstrate the sensitivity of government finances to changes in macroeconomic performance, they do not allow for the possibility that the high level of debt may itself adversely affect macroeconomic performance. Perhaps one of the most important channels by which this can occur is that high government deficits and debt levels lead to financial markets demanding a risk premium on government debt, which has the effect of raising the real cost of capital throughout the economy. As discussed in the monetary policy section, there is evidence that the reduction in the interest premium, which has occurred as a result of the improved inflation performance since the late 1980s, has been largely offset by the effect of increased budget deficits.

In order to provide some tentative quantitative guidance as to the scale of the potential long-term benefits from fiscal consolidation, the estimated relationship linking real long-term interest rates and the size of budget deficits discussed in the monetary policy section has been incorporated into the OECD Secretariat's INTERLINK model (see Annex V). A number of variants of the same basic simulation are considered.[16] In the absence of any fall in long-term interest rates, fiscal consolidation leads to a temporary short-term reduction in GDP, but in the long run GDP recovers and is unchanged on a cumulative basis (the effect of a tighter fiscal stance being offset by a looser monetary policy). However, if allowance is made for the likely reduction in real long-term interest rates, then although fiscal consolidation initially leads to a similar temporary loss in GDP, within four years activity has recovered to its baseline level and after seven years there are positive gains in output on a cumulative basis (see Figure 20). These long-term gains are a direct consequence of the beneficial supply-side effect of reduced real long-term interest rates on the cost-of-capital and, in turn, increased investment and productive capacity. Positive gains to GDP are realised more quickly if the fall in long-term interest rates is immediate rather than being delayed over a number of years: in this case, GDP is above the baseline after only

51

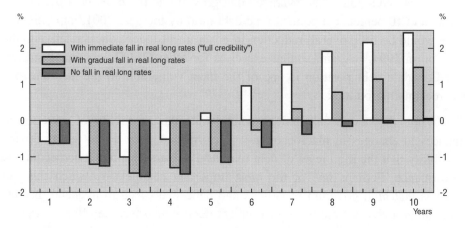

Figure 20. **EFFECT ON CUMULATIVE GDP OF FISCAL RETRENCHMENT**
Cumulative GDP (percentage point years)

With immediate fall in real long rates ("full credibility")
With gradual fall in real long rates
No fall in real long rates

Note: This figure shows the cumulative effect on GDP from a cut in government current expenditure by 1 per cent of GDP, using the OECD Secretariat's INTERLINK model.
For further details of the simulation see the discussion in the text and in Annex V.
Source: OECD Secretariat.

three years and by the fifth year the cumulative output loss of the first two years has been made good. Such a scenario would reflect a situation where financial markets, firms and households regard fiscal consolidation plans as being fully credible from the outset.

The general qualitative conclusion following from these simulation exercises, namely that further fiscal retrenchment is likely to involve some short-term loss in output which would be more than made up over the medium term, is supported by Canadian research.[17] Another common finding is that the short-term pain of deficit reduction is likely to be smaller the greater the credibility of such a plan since this will imply a quicker response from interest rates. In addition, further fiscal retrenchment could have a beneficial effect on macroeconomic policy-making by providing greater room for manoeuvre in counter-cyclical fiscal policy, by under-pinning the credibility of official commitments to low inflation, and by leading to greater stability in the exchange rate.

In the absence of additional consolidation, high debt levels may inhibit counter-cyclical fiscal policy actions and so lead to greater volatility in the business cycle, since further increases in debt may cause lenders to demand higher risk premia, so raising the risk that debt levels will rise permanently. Indeed, there does seem to be evidence both for Canada, as well as some other major OECD economies, that counter-cyclical fiscal policy action was more restrained than normal during the most recent downturn.[18] Further efforts to reduce the budget deficit would also help to convince financial markets and other economic agents that the authorities have no intention to deal with the outstanding debt burden by resorting to inflation and so enhance the credibility of the current monetary policy framework discussed above.

This would be all the more useful given that rising public debt has been reflected in increasing foreign indebtedness. The ratio of net external liabilities to GDP for Canada was 45½ per cent of GDP in 1994, which is high in comparison with most other OECD countries (see Figure 21). The magnitude of this debt, together with the burden of debt service it places on the current account, may lead to greater volatility in the exchange rate. Although Canada's net international investment position has been traditionally in substantial deficit, the fact

Figure 21. **NET EXTERNAL DEBT**[1]
Per cent of GDP

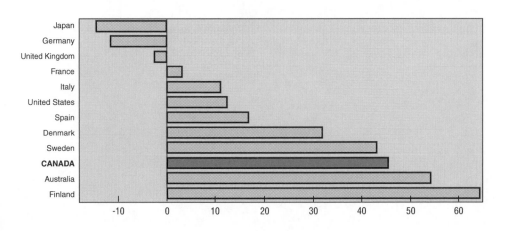

1. 1993. For United Kingdom, United States, Finland and Canada, 1994.
Source: OECD Secretariat.

53

that governments – in particular the provinces – have recently increasingly relied on the issue of foreign debt has certainly contributed to exchange market nervousness. Almost half of externally held Canadian bonds originate from provinces and foreign holdings now account for more than 40 per cent of the outstanding stock of provincial debt. Further fiscal action, particularly at the provincial level, to reduce the stock of foreign debt and thus debt service costs, might help to relieve pressure on the balance of payments, and in turn, on the exchange rate.

In summary, sustained fiscal consolidation efforts should eventually develop a virtuous circle of debt dynamics, whereby lower deficits and debt lead to lower debt service and reduced risk premia, thus inducing a further deficit reduction. In view of long-term pressures from pension commitments and health care programmes,[19] which will rise as the population ages, it is all the more critical that addressing the current problem of fiscal imbalance remains a top priority.

III. Progress in structural reform

With a view to ensuring better growth and employment performance, the new government launched a comprehensive review process in several structural policy areas after taking office in late 1993. In some cases, notably social security and indirect taxation, reforms have yet to be implemented, but the government has issued proposals which are discussed here. This chapter focuses on labour market reforms in the light of the recommendations in the recent OECD "Jobs Study". Initiatives associated with industrial policy are dealt with separately in Chapter IV.

Labour markets

Recommendations of the OECD Jobs Study

One of the central recommendations of the recent OECD Jobs Study, namely *"Reform unemployment and related benefit systems such that societies' fundamental equity goals are achieved in ways that impinge far less on the efficient functioning of labour markets"* is very pertinent to Canada, as a major reform of the unemployment-insurance (UI) is currently being considered there. Moreover, since UI is self-financing on the basis of employer and employee premiums, any resulting savings could eventually lead to a reduction in payroll taxes which would be consistent with another recommendation of the Jobs Study to *"Reduce non-wage labour costs, by reducing taxes on labour (where the budget situation or expenditure reductions make this possible)..."*. Alternatively, reform of the UI system could also be used to redirect resources in line with a further recommendation of the Jobs Study to *"Expand and enhance active labour market policies ... to shift the focus of labour market policies from the passive provision of income support to more active measures"*. The following discussion summarises the evidence on the distortions which the current UI system introduces into the Canadian labour market and then goes on to consider recent government proposals for reform, including how any savings might best be used. A more extended discussion of the UI system can be found in Chapter III of last year's OECD Survey of Canada.

Problems with the system of Unemployment Insurance

Two inter-related characteristics of the Canadian UI system stand out as causing distortions to the labour market and are therefore deserving attention in the context of future reforms: firstly, the regionally-extended nature of benefits aggravates regional unemployment differences; secondly, the system encourages a high incidence of frequent users.

The UI system allows for more generous benefits (in terms of longer periods of benefit entitlement and easier entrance requirements) in regions of above-average unemployment. The dependence of the system's generosity on fluctuations in regional unemployment rates may be partly responsible for the persistence of regional unemployment differences observed over the last two decades. Both the *Royal Commission on the Economic Union and Development Prospects for Canada* (1985) and the *Commission of Inquiry on Unemployment Insurance* (1986) have recommended that regional differentiation of the programme be ended. Subsequent empirical studies, reviewed in last year's OECD Survey of Canada, tend to reinforce the view that the regional differentiation of the programme has substantial costs.

A characteristic of the UI system which has been singled out for criticism is its propensity to encourage repeat-use, so that a significant and growing proportion of the workforce rely on UI as a regular form of income supplement. This problem also has a distinct regional dimension. It is partly caused by a feature of the Canadian system which stands out in comparisons across OECD countries, namely that in high unemployment regions relatively brief periods of employment qualify individuals for relatively long periods of benefit eligibility. Repeat-users are therefore much more common in regions with above-average unemployment rates and also in industries characterised by seasonal work (for example construction and primary industries). Thus, 38 per cent of UI recipients were repeat-users in 1991, *i.e.* those with at least three claims over a five-year period, with this proportion rising to between 53 and 68 per cent in the Atlantic provinces. Moreover, the situation may be worsening over time as empirical evidence suggests that the mean duration of claims rises with repeat use, while the amount of time between claims falls.

A number of macroeconomic studies have found the change in the UI system in 1971 (when there was a substantial increase in its generosity) led to a significant increase in the non-accelerating inflation rate of unemployment (NAIRU) of the order of 2 percentage points.[20] Subsequent modifications to the UI system, which have reduced its overall level of generosity, may not have reversed this effect to the extent that they have exacerbated differences in generosity across the provinces.[21] Nevertheless, the reforms in the 1994 Budget, which reduced both the overall generosity of the system as well as inter-provincial differences in this regard, should unambiguously contribute to a decline in the NAIRU.

A recent review of studies attempting to explain changes in the NAIRU in Canada concluded that the main cause of its renewed rise in the early 1990s was the substantial increase in payroll taxes.[22, 23] There remains some disagreement as to whether changes in payroll taxes have a permanent or temporary effect on the NAIRU.[24] However, even if it is "temporary", it is likely that the effect on unemployment is of a magnitude and duration sufficient to constitute a major issue of policy concern.[25] Moreover, to the extent that changes in the payroll tax have only a temporary effect on the NAIRU, it is the rate of increase in such a tax rather than its overall level, which may be the better indicator of potential harm to the labour market. Indeed, the increase in payroll taxes (as well as total taxes on labour costs, including income taxes) in recent years has been among the most severe of the major seven OECD economies, as shown in Figure 22, Panel A – even though the absolute level of such taxes remains comparatively low[26] (Panel B).

Current policies and proposals for further reform of the UI system

In response to growing dissatisfaction with its operation as well as its escalating cost in the context of increasing need for fiscal discipline, governments have progressively reduced the generosity of the UI system through a process of marginal changes to the main parameters of the system. For example, reforms introduced in the 1994 Budget increased the minimum period of work required to qualify for UI benefits, reduced the maximum duration of benefits and lowered the benefit rate (except for low-income beneficiaries).[27] Moreover, the reduction

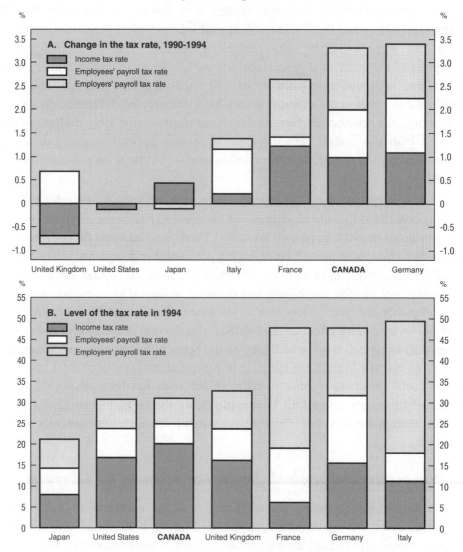

Figure 22. **THE TAX RATE ON LABOUR COSTS
IN THE MAJOR OECD COUNTRIES**

Percentage of annual gross labour costs

Notes: The tax rate is calculated as the sum of income tax, and employees' and employers' payroll taxes paid on gross labour costs (gross earnings plus employers' payroll taxes) for the average production worker.
Source: The Tax/Benefit Position of the Average Production Worker, OECD, Paris.

in generosity (in terms of qualifying period and maximum duration of benefits) was greatest for the high unemployment regions, so that it implied a further reduction in regional differentiation of the system.[28] Nevertheless, the generosity of the system in high unemployment regions, in terms of the minimum qualifying period and maximum duration of benefits, remains significant in comparison with other OECD economies.

In October 1994 the government issued a discussion paper,[29] including the outline of proposals which would represent a more comprehensive reform of the UI system, rather than a continuation of previous incremental changes to the system. A central feature of these proposals is an explicit distinction between occasional and frequent claimants. Under the proposals, occasional users would receive assistance on a similar basis to the present system. Frequent users, however, would receive lower benefits, combined with more active assistance in finding a job. Moreover, income support for frequent users could be means-tested and possibly conditional on participation in training programmes.

The discussion paper proposals were subjected to a thorough review process. The House of Commons Human Resources Committee, a working group set up by the government to examine issues related to seasonable work, and most provincial governments expressed their concerns regarding the two-tier proposal to address the problem of frequent claimants. Nevertheless, the federal government is committed to introducing some changes to the UI system later this year. The 1995 Budget plan assumes that implementation of such changes will begin no later than mid-1996 and, together with the effect of improvements in the economy on the labour market, the overall size of the unemployment insurance programme will be reduced by C\$ 700 million in 1996/97 and by at least 10 per cent by the year 2000.

Although it now seems that a two-tier system which explicitly distinguishes frequent from occasional users has been ruled out, modifications to the current scheme are, nevertheless, likely to be implemented to address the structural problems inherent in the current programme design, including the issue of frequent claimants. Among proposals under discussion are the reduction in the benefit rate according to the extent of previous UI usage by the claimant and the extension of the period over which average earnings are taken into account for the purpose of benefit calculation. Further changes to the main parameters of the existing UI system, along the lines of those made in the 1994 Budget, would only tackle the main structural problems of the system indirectly. In addition, in such a case, benefits would be reduced for all claimants, including those who have not previously accessed the system.

The proposals in the discussion paper also envisaged that some of the savings from UI reform might be used to finance increased expenditure on employment development services, which are taken to encompass a wide range of activities including job counselling, provision of labour market information, the enhancement of basic skills such as literacy, classroom and on-the-job training, and wage subsidies for the long-term unemployed. However, the proposals are not clear as to what proportion of any savings in the UI programme should be directed towards active labour market measures as opposed to being used to finance a reduction in payroll taxes.

Should savings be spent on active measures?

There would seem to be a case for some increased expenditure on active measures in line with the OECD Jobs Study recommendations, given the high proportion of labour market expenditure currently on passive measures. However, as shown in Table 13, Canada is the median country among the major seven

Table 13. **Public expenditure on labour market programmes**

Percentage of GDP[1]

Programme category	Canada (1994/95)	France (1993)	Germany (1994)	Italy (1992)	Japan (1993/94)	United Kingdom (1993/94)	United States (1993/94)
1. Employment services and administration	0.21	0.15	0.24	0.08	0.03	0.24	0.08
2. Labour market training	0.37	0.44	0.42	0.02	0.03	0.16	0.07
3. Youth measures	0.02	0.28	0.06	0.80	–	0.14	0.04
4. Subsidised employment	0.04	0.26	0.34	–	0.03	0.02	0.01
5. Measures for the disabled	–	0.08	0.26	–	–	0.03	0.05
6. Unemployment compensation	1.56	1.72	2.03	0.62	0.32	1.59	0.45
7. Early retirement for labour market reasons	0.01	0.38	0.49	0.26	–	–	–
Total	2.20	3.31	3.84	1.77	0.41	2.18	0.69
Total active measures (1 to 5)	0.63	1.21	1.32	0.90	0.09	0.59	0.24
Total passive measures (6 to 7)	1.57	2.10	2.52	0.87	0.32	1.59	0.45

1. Data are shown for latest year for which they are available.
Source: OECD, *Employment Outlook*, July 1995.

60

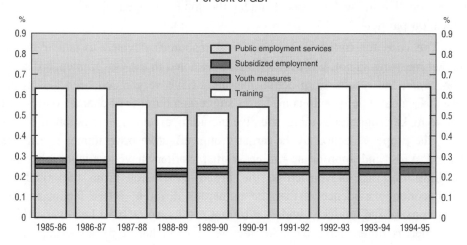

Figure 23. **EXPENDITURE ON ACTIVE LABOUR MARKET MEASURES**
Per cent of GDP

Source: OECD, *Employment Outlook.*

OECD countries in terms of spending on active measures as a percentage of GDP. Moreover, in recent years the expenditure on active measures, especially training, has been significantly increased (see Figure 23).[30]

To the extent that active labour market measures are broadly defined (as they are in the government's discussion paper) to include improving labour force skills, there would seem to be some scope for action to deal with particular weaknesses in the Canadian labour market which stand out in international comparisons. For example, employed Canadians with low qualification levels receive the lowest of job-related continuing education and training compared with other OECD countries. In addition, several indicators, including unemployment rates, point to school-to-work transition being a problem area. However, recent federal youth initiatives have been aimed at addressing this issue and appear to be having some success. For example, under Youth Internship Canada, the federal government provides seed funding to encourage industry and education institutions to develop structured pathways from school to emerging and expanding sectors of the economy. Industry and education partners come together to develop relevant training curricula which combine in-class with on-the-job training and which are based on industry-determined skill standards. Where

61

programmes have been developed, it is expected that they will remain in place once federal funding has ceased, under the joint management of industry and education partners.

The case for further increasing total resources devoted to active labour market measures is not, however, clearcut. As noted in the Government's discussion paper, the results from active measures have very much been a "hit-or-miss". Evaluation of previous measures suggests a number of characteristics that tend to make programmes more effective including precise specification of objectives, the proper selection of the target group, effective programmes to involve needed skills, and appropriate timing so that workers have available jobs after finishing training. Nevertheless, the broad conclusion from the available microeconomic evidence is that the numerous different active labour market programmes have produced widely different results; some have been very effective whereas others have been ineffective or even had a negative impact on participants' labour market performance. Moreover, there is little compelling macroeconomic evidence to indicate that, in aggregate, active job measures have had a measurably positive impact on the labour market. In contrast, as discussed above, there is strong evidence at the macroeconomic level that payroll taxes have had an adverse effect on employment. This would suggest that the opportunity cost of any further expansion in the total resources devoted to active labour market policies (for example, from savings in the UI system) should be carefully assessed against the more certain benefit from lower payroll taxes. In any case, further expansion in the total resources devoted to active labour market policies should be directed to those programmes which have produced results. The federal government's goal is to have a flexible range of tested programme options, backed by research and information, so that, at the local level, individuals together with programme staff and community partners can choose the most appropriate intervention.

Assessment

In summary, it is to be hoped that measures to reform the present UI system along the lines discussed above, will be introduced in the coming year and so address its most obvious weaknesses. Nevertheless, further reforms, particularly to reduce the regional differentiation in the generosity of the UI programme, may need to be considered in future. The case for using the savings from reform of the

UI system to increase overall expenditure on active labour market measures needs to be carefully weighed against the evidence of the likely gains from a reduction in payroll taxes.

It should, however, be noted that discussion as to whether any savings from reform of the UI system should be spent on active measures or reductions in payroll taxes is all predicated on the assumption that the former are financed from the UI account and on the current requirement that UI is self-financing. Although active labour market measures which are targeted at UI recipients are currently financed from the UI account, other measures which aim at the wider population are financed from general taxation. However, in practice this distinction between measures may not be clear-cut and having different sources of funding for different programmes may lead to a lack of co-ordination. Moreover, to the extent that further active measures are worthwhile, it is not clear why they should be dependent on sufficient savings being generated from reform of the UI system (or on higher payroll taxes, which on the available evidence seem to be particularly damaging to employment). More generally, financing UI from general taxation at the margin would avoid the situation of a severe cyclical downturn leading to job losses, not only from a reduction in demand but also from the effect of the increased payroll taxes required to keep the UI account balanced. A possible alternative solution to this problem, which was raised in the above-mentioned discussion paper and is favoured by the government, would be to build up surpluses in the UI account during cyclical upturns, which would then be depleted during downturns. However, such an approach would require the government to be able to correctly forecast the strength of future business cycles.

Programme review

As noted in Chapter II, a Programme Review was announced in the 1994 Budget as a means to reduce the overall cost of government and to focus expenditures on highest priority activities, with the results being incorporated in the 1995 Budget. To undertake this review, Ministers were asked to apply six tests to their programmes and services: the extent to which they serve the public interest; the necessity of government involvement (as opposed to the private sector); appropriateness of the federal role (as opposed to other levels of government), scope for public sector/private sector partnerships; scope for increased efficiency; and affordability.

The Programme Review has led to structural changes in what the federal government does in Canada and how it delivers its programmes and services. The review encompassed about C$ 52 billion worth of spending, excluding only major statutory transfers, and achieved savings equivalent to nearly 20 per cent of total departmental expenditure, with some ministries having their budget cut by nearly half (Figure 24). In some cases (most notably transportation), it also led to policies which can be considered as moving ahead the agenda for structural reform. The Programme Review's key achievements include:

- The elimination or substantial reduction of subsidies (see Chapter II for further details).
- The redesign of programmes to make them more efficient and cost-effective: for example, regional development agencies will no longer be involved in the provision of grants and subsidies and instead will act as regional delivery offices for federal programmes in their relevant areas.
- The merger or consolidation of programmes: for instance, operations and equipment will be integrated among some departments, while various labour market programmes are now rationalised under one umbrella.
- The devolution of programmes or activities to other levels of government, such as the management of freshwater habitat which will be transferred to provinces, and that of airports which will be shifted to local authorities.
- The commercialisation or privatisation of activities: in particular, the remaining government interest in Petro-Canada will be sold, Canadian National (railways) will be privatised, and Transport Canada's Air Navigation System will be commercialised.

The 1995 Budget also announced a major reform to the management of government expenditures, introducing the new Expenditure Management System. Under this system, there will be no reserves for new policy initiatives and all new spending will have to come from internal reallocations of resources either from within or among the relevant Ministries. As part of the System, Departments will be required to submit three-year business plans. These plans will provide a strategic focus to future departmental activities that will be undertaken given

Figure 24. **CHANGES IN FEDERAL DEPARTMENTAL SPENDING**
1997-98 relative to 1994-95

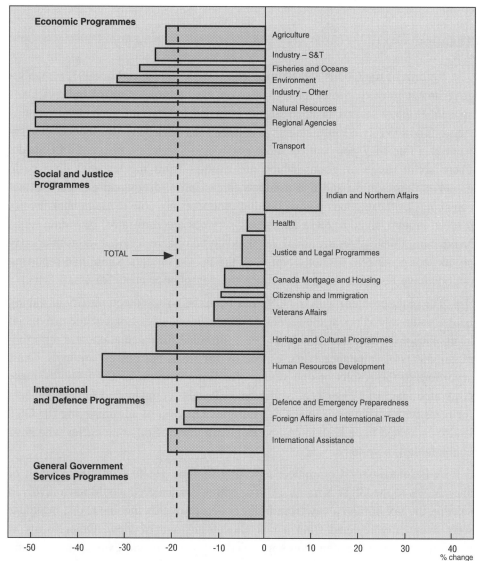

% change   % change

Note: The width of each bar is proportional to the programme expenditure in 1994-95, the length is proportional to the percentage change between 1994-95 and 1997-98 as a result of the Programme Review.
Source: Department of Finance, *Budget 1995*.

65

approved expenditure levels. The business plans will be for the first time scrutinised by Parliamentary Committee, helping to ensure that planning is long term, strategic and open to public comment.

Taxation

Reform of the Goods and Service Tax (GST), introduced in 1991, remains a government priority. However, progress on the harmonisation of indirect taxes appears to have stalled in negotiations between federal and provincial governments. The GST is a multi-stage value-added tax levied by the federal government at a rate of 7 per cent on most goods and services consumed in Canada. There are a range of goods which are exempt from the tax including basic groceries, agricultural and fish products, prescription drugs and exports (so that consumers of these goods pay no tax and producers are able to claim back the tax paid on inputs). In addition, a number of services are zero-rated, including rents, health care, financial, educational, legal aid and day-care services (consumers pay no tax, but producers cannot claim back the tax on inputs). Simplified reporting options have been introduced to reduce the compliance costs for small firms.

The main problem with the GST has been the cost and complexity of having both a value-added tax at the federal level and retail sales taxes at the provincial level, each with different tax bases, rates, formulae for calculation, and reporting requirements. Compliance costs, especially for small businesses, are high. Thus, according to the results of one study,[31] for firms with under C$ 100 000, these costs amounted to 17 per cent of the tax collected, compared to only 3 per cent for firms with revenues of over C$ 1 million. The cost of administering the GST is also estimated to be high in comparison with those of other countries who have comparable tax systems.

A Parliamentary Committee, reporting in June 1994, examined a range of alternatives to the GST. A number of the options considered would have involved shifting the tax burden away from indirect taxes towards income taxes, but these were eventually rejected from a risk-allocation point of view. Other forms of possible taxation on expenditures included a direct personal expenditure tax and a business transfer tax, although the Committee was concerned that administrative and compliance costs of these alternatives would have been as high as for the GST and that their introduction would also incur disruption and transition costs.[32]

Ultimately, the Committee recommended an integrated federal-provincial value-added tax, along with measures to reduce compliance costs for small businesses. In the fall of 1994, federal and provincial governments suggested approaches for harmonisation. The federal proposal was for a harmonised value-added tax at a single national rate of 12 per cent of which 5 per cent would be for the federal government (as compared to the current rate of 7 per cent).

However, a number of provinces have rejected the federal proposal of harmonisation. Widely differing indirect tax systems at the provincial level underlie this lack of enthusiasm. For example, one province (Alberta) has no sales tax and only Quebec already has a form of value-added tax (although it is not completely harmonised with the federal GST). The proposed federal lower single rate could imply significant loss of revenue to some provinces, which have high sales tax rates and/or rely heavily on the taxation of business inputs (that are not subject to tax under a value-added system). Provinces might also be wary of the disruption which such a transition could cause. In October 1994, Ontario alternatively proposed that the provinces abandon indirect taxes altogether, allowing the federal government to implement any reform as it chose. In return, the federal government would give up an equivalent amount of room in the income tax field, as well as enabling the provinces to make changes in the income tax base. Differences between the federal and provincial positions have yet to be resolved, although the newly-elected provincial government in Ontario seems to be more receptive to harmonisation proposals than its predecessor.

There could be substantial gains in economic efficiency from a move towards harmonisation and the consequent shift in the incidence of provincial taxes away from intermediate inputs (on which the provincial sales taxes are heavily based) and towards consumption. It would also imply a reduction both in the costs of compliance and in tax administration. A further reduction in such costs as well as increased simplification would be achieved if the tax base were broadened.

International and interprovincial trade

The North American Free Trade Agreement (NAFTA)

From the beginning of 1994 the NAFTA, including Mexico, effectively replaces the Canada-US Free Trade Agreement (FTA) incorporating the latter's basic elements (see Chapter IV). The new agreement provides for the elimination of all tariffs between Canada and Mexico over a period of ten years. Furthermore, all three countries are committed to extending national treatment to investors from the other partner countries.

Both the FTA and NAFTA have boosted Canada's trade with the United States. Estimates of the overall income gain to Canada from the FTA are typically in the range of 2^1/$_2$ to 3^1/$_2$ per cent of GDP. Assessing the effect of the NAFTA on trade with Mexico is more difficult. There was a substantial increase in merchandise exports to Mexico of nearly 30 per cent between 1993 and 1994, so that Mexico's share of total Canadian exports rose to about 4 per cent in 1994, while Canadian imports from Mexico increased by 20 per cent in 1994. However, it remains to be seen whether these gains are sustained following the massive devaluation of the peso at the end of 1994. The first round of accelerated tariff elimination under NAFTA, initiated in January 1994, is still under way. Although negotiations have proceeded slowly for a number of reasons, including the Mexican financial crisis and the sensitivity of the products under consideration, they have now resumed and it is hoped that the round will be completed in the near future.

In December 1994 at the Summit of the Americas, negotiations to extend the NAFTA to Chile were announced. The effect on trade with Canada is not expected to be great as Chile is not a large trading partner, although it is an important destination for Canadian foreign direct investment. The intention to create a hemispheric free trade zone by the year 2005 was also announced at the summit. In addition, Canada is a signatory to the November 1994 agreement on Asian-Pacific Economic Cooperation (APEC), which envisages the creation of a Pacific free trade and investment zone by 2020.

The Uruguay Round

The Uruguay round agreement was approved by the Canadian Parliament in November 1994 for implementation at the beginning of 1995 (although the introduction of provisions did not occur until August. Under the agreement Canadian tariffs will be reduced by an average of about one-third, with industrial tariffs falling by about half. In addition, Canada will eliminate tariffs on a wide range of goods including paper and paper products, construction equipment, agricultural equipment, medical equipment, steel, pharmaceuticals, office furniture, beer, whisky and brandies. Canada will benefit from tariff reductions abroad on industrial exports, with Japan reducing such tariffs by an average of 56 per cent, and the European Union by 37 per cent.

The sector which is likely to be most affected is agriculture, with Canada reducing agricultural tariffs in this area by an average of 36 per cent and a minimum of 15 per cent per item. Furthermore, in accordance with the WTO Agreement on Agriculture, all import restrictions have been converted to tariff-rate quotas (TRQs) which represent Canada's minimum access commitments under the Agreement. Imports exceeding the TRQs will be subject to a higher rate. The Agreement also requires Canada to reduce trade-distorting domestic subsidies in the agricultural sector, although much progress (relative to the historical levels prevailing in 1986-88 specified as the benchmark in the Agreement) had already been made in this field. In August 1995, Canada eliminated the annual railway subsidy of C\$ 560 million under the Western Grain Transportation Act.

Overall, the likely impact of Uruguay Round Agreement on Canada is expected to be relatively small because trade with the United States (which accounts for about 80 per cent of Canadian trade in goods) has already been substantially liberalised under the FTA (see above). The Department of Finance[33] estimate that the Uruguay Agreement could eventually increase GDP by the order of $1/2$ per cent of GDP as a result of increased demand for Canadian exports, which in turn reflects higher global income, particularly from Canada's non-traditional trading partners.

The Internal Trade Agreement

In July 1994, the Prime Minister and provincial premiers signed an agreement to reduce inter-provincial trade barriers. Internal trade in Canada is almost as large as Canada's international trade, being equivalent to nearly one-third of GDP. However, a wide range of non-tariff barriers to internal trade have existed, particularly in the form of standards, regulations and government procurement practices. Estimates of the cost of these barriers vary widely, but their negative effect on resource allocation is likely to be substantial. The aim of the Agreement on Internal Trade is to reduce such barriers, with specific obligations in ten economic sectors, including government procurement, labour mobility and investment.

The opening up of government procurement practices is perhaps the most important sector covered by the agreement. From July 1995, procurement by provinces and other major public agencies will be open to out-of-province suppliers. Ultimately the agreement will cover contracts worth about C$ 50 billion per annum, with expected savings of between C$ 2 billion and C$ 6 billion per annum as a result of increased competition. Other provisions of the agreement include: elimination of residency requirements for employment or licensing; mutual recognition of occupational qualifications and licensing systems; prohibition of the use of safety or environmental standards to discriminate against out-of-province suppliers; a prohibition on provincial investment incentives designed to compete with other provinces; a prohibition on the creation of new trade barriers; and the establishment of a formal dispute resolution mechanism. The agreement represents an important first step to freeing up inter-provincial trade, but further progress needs to be made, particularly in the more contentious areas such as agriculture and energy (although a deadline of July was set for reaching an agreement regarding energy).

IV. Industrial performance and policies

Canada's industrial structure has long been a focus for policymakers given their concern to improve productivity and real income levels, as well as the country's ability to compete in international markets. Behind this focus, there have been several broad and enduring preoccupations. Perhaps most prominent has been the perception that Canadian companies are less innovative than their international rivals – the "innovation gap" – and that, consequently, rates of technological change have been unduly slow in Canadian domestic industries. A related concern has been that economic activity in Canada is strongly concentrated in natural resources and resource-based primary manufacturing industries which arguably are less susceptible to technological change and productivity improvements.

The attention paid to the industrial features of the Canadian economy has changed over time, however. In the 1980s, deregulation and free trade emerged as prominent and controversial initiatives designed to promote changes in Canada's industrial structure, while industrial concentration and inward foreign direct investment, which had dominated the debate in the 1970s, became much less central in the public policy arena. More recently, concerns about international competitiveness have focused on promoting a healthy market place, improving Canada's infrastructure, both physical and non-physical, exploiting internal and external trade opportunities as well as the development and diffusion of technology and innovation throughout the economy (particularly in small and medium-sized businesses).

A number of changes in the economic environment, which have tended to increase international competition, have also highlighted the necessity for Canadian industries to "restructure": rapid evolution towards a globally-integrated economy, due to advances in communications and transportation as well as to reductions in trade and investment barriers in the context of the Free Trade

71

Agreement with the United States; increased production capacity in developing and newly-industrialised economies; and a revolution in technology, especially in microelectronics that has put knowledge and information at the cutting edge of economic progress.[34] These trends are the backdrop for the present Government's industrial strategy, which focuses on building a more innovative economy. By inducing the authorities to use public resources more efficiently, the need to tackle the budget deficit has also contributed to the new approach to industrial policy.

The present chapter first briefly describes the structure of Canada's industry and assesses its recent record. It then attempts to evaluate possible impediments to better industrial performance and reviews the related policy response. This is followed by a discussion of the current government strategy and future priorities to promote industrial restructuring.

Key features of Canada's industrial developments

Before reviewing evidence on Canada's industrial performance and considering various explanations of the observed developments, it is useful to provide a brief description of the main characteristics of the country's industrial structure with a view to illustrating the concerns underlying current government policies.

Structure

Sectoral composition

Canada is a mature economy, with the bulk of its activity now derived from the tertiary sector. From 1961 to 1994, the share of real GDP originating in the resource extraction, construction and manufacturing sectors declined from around 40 to 34 per cent (Figure 25). These sectors lost ground primarily to finance, insurance and real estate. Changes in the shares of GDP originating in other sectors were relatively modest. The trends observed are similar to those in the United States and other OECD countries, with the manufacturing sector's share declining more slowly, albeit from a relatively low level.[35]

A more detailed look at the sectoral composition of the Canadian manufacturing sector (Table 14) shows that high value-added secondary manufacturing industries (such as electrical equipment, chemicals, etc.) have a lower weight

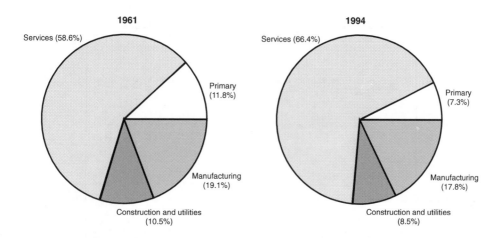

Figure 25. **SECTORAL COMPOSITION OF THE CANADIAN ECONOMY**
Per cent of GDP volume

1961

Services (58.6%)

Primary
(11.8%)

Manufacturing
(19.1%)

Construction and utilities
(10.5%)

1994

Services (66.4%)

Primary
(7.3%)

Manufacturing
(17.8%)

Construction and utilities
(8.5%)

Source: Statistics Canada.

than on average in the OECD, and in particular in the United States, with the notable exception of motor vehicle production. Conversely, resource-based primary industries (in particular, wood and food) account for a high share of manufacturing value added by international comparison. This relative concentration on primary manufacturing along with the low share of high-technology industries underlies some of the concerns about Canada's industrial structure.

Mirroring these structural features, the data in Table 15 on the distribution of Canadian merchandise exports and imports for seven broadly-defined industrial sectors further underscore the relatively low representation of high value-added industrial activities in Canada, as well as those with strong technological linkages to other industrial sectors. This has contributed to the chronic large trade deficit in machinery and equipment. Similarly, the trade surplus in the resource and forestry sectors reflects to some extent a relatively high concentration on ''low technology'' activities.

Table 14. Share of manufacturing value added by industry[1]

Current prices, per cent

Industry	Canada	United States	France	Germany	Italy	Japan	United Kingdom	OECD[2]
Food, drink and tobacco	14.4	11.0	13.2	10.6	10.8	10.6	20.2	14.3
Textiles, footwear, leather	5.4	5.0	6.0	3.6	16.1	4.6	5.1	5.4
Wood, cork, furniture	6.4	4.6	3.3	3.3	5.7	2.7	3.5	4.6
Paper and printing	15.5	11.5	7.9	4.7	6.2	7.7	10.1	10.6
Chemicals	13.6	17.4	19.6	17.5	12.8	13.0	13.0	15.2
Industrial chemicals	6.6	8.5	7.1	8.1	..	5.7	6.1	7.2
Pharmaceuticals	2.1	3.2	1.8	1.9	..	2.3	2.6	2.1
Petroleum refining	1.5	1.8	6.6	3.5	1.1	0.8	1.0	2.5
Rubber and plastic products	3.4	3.8	4.1	3.9	4.9	4.2	3.3	3.6
Stone, clay, glass	3.2	2.4	4.2	3.9	7.3	3.5	4.3	4.0
Basic metal industries	6.2	4.3	4.7	7.0	3.8	7.6	3.1	6.0
Ferrous metals	3.1	2.7	3.2	4.9	3.1	5.7	2.3	3.5
Non-ferrous metals	3.1	1.6	1.5	2.1	0.7	1.9	0.8	2.4
Fabricated metal products and machinery	32.7	41.9	39.6	48.8	36.2	46.3	36.9	38.3
Fabricated metal products	5.5	6.5	7.5	9.9	10.4	6.2	4.8	7.6
Non-electrical machinery	6.4	7.9	6.8	10.0	8.5	9.6	8.3	8.4
Office machines and computers	1.0	2.7	2.4	2.1	1.0	3.6	2.5	1.8
Electrical machinery	2.9	2.5	5.3	5.5	4.3	6.7	3.7	3.8
Communications equipment	3.7	5.9	4.7	6.5	2.8	8.9	5.2	5.0
Shipbuilding	0.5	0.7	0.5	0.3	0.4	0.6	0.8	1.1
Motor vehicles	9.3	4.5	7.7	11.0	4.6	8.6	4.3	6.2
Aerospace	2.8	5.5	2.6	1.0	1.1	0.2	4.1	2.0
Other transport equipment	0.7	0.2	0.5	0.2	0.9	0.3	0.3	0.4
Instruments	0.0	5.5	1.6	2.2	2.3	1.6	2.9	2.0
Other manufacturing	2.5	1.8	1.5	0.7	1.1	3.8	3.9	1.7
High-technology	12.4	25.3	18.4	19.2	14.1	23.3	20.9	19.1
Resource-intensive	28.7	21.4	28.8	23.4	25.2	19.6	29.7	25.3

1. 1991. Canada 1990.
2. Unweighted average.
Source: OECD, STAN database.

74

Table 15.   **Composition of merchandise trade**

1994, balance of payments basis

	Exports		Imports	
	C$ billion	Per cent	C$ billion	Per cent
Agriculture and fish products	17.6	8.1	12.6	6.4
Energy products	21.7	10.0	7.1	3.6
Forest products	31.2	14.3	1.8	0.9
Industrial goods	39.4	18.1	38.7	19.6
Machines and equipment	43.0	19.8	65.6	33.3
Automobile products	58.4	26.9	47.8	24.3
Consumer goods	5.8	2.7	23.5	11.9

Source: Statistics Canada.

Concentration and ownership

Canadian industries have traditionally been characterised by relatively high levels of concentration and foreign ownership. At the same time, Canadian-owned companies tend to be relatively small by international standards. Levels of concentration are significant on both an individual industry and aggregate basis. For example, the 25 largest enterprises (ranked by assets) controlled almost 46 per cent of all assets in 1992; however, among Canadian-owned companies, only two ranked among the world's 200 largest companies.[36] The share of foreign controlled assets was around 24 per cent in 1992 for all non-financial industries and approximately 17 per cent for the finance and insurance sector. Within the non-financial sector, foreign control of assets ranged from less than 5 per cent for transportation services to over 66 per cent for chemicals, chemical products and textiles. US investors accounted for almost 60 per cent of foreign-controlled assets in non-financial industries and approximately 37 per cent of such assets in the finance and insurance sector.[37] A number of US-owned companies are among the largest ones in Canada.

Despite numerous privatisations since the mid-1980s, there is still a relatively high degree of government ownership of business enterprises, at least in comparison with the United States. The number of federal crown corporations has fallen from around 90 to 50, but in addition there are hundreds of provincial crown corporations.[38] There is also a large number of "mixed" enterprises where a government or government agency owns voting shares of a business enterprise along with non-governmental individuals or organisations. It is estimated that, in 1992, governments accounted for almost 16 per cent of all domestically-controlled assets in the non-financial sector and approximately 8 per cent of those in the finance and insurance sector.[39]

Performance

Productivity

The productivity performance of the economy, and of the industrial sector in particular, has been a major concern for Canadian policy makers. A detailed analysis in the 1991/92 OECD Economic Survey of Canada identified a number of factors (notably a greater intensity of industrial energy use and the discontinu-ation of special factors that had boosted trade) which might explain the more pronounced slowdown in the growth of total factor productivity (TFP) – *i.e.* out-put growth not accounted for by additional labour and capital inputs – than generally experienced elsewhere. Poor TFP performance has persisted, however, despite the structural reforms implemented since the mid-1980s.

Canada, even more than other major countries, did not share the surge in productivity growth experienced by the United States in the second half of the 1980s. As a result, the productivity shortfall relative to the United States widened significantly, while Canada's productivity advantage *vis-à-vis* the other major OECD countries diminished. With continued weak performance in the early 1990s, Canada's TFP changed little from 1979 to 1994, according to OECD Secretariat estimates (Table 16). It is too early to say whether a recent increase (Figure 26) signals a structural shift rather than a cyclical pick-up. Adjusted for capacity utilisation, TFP has also shown some improvement but appears to have remained below the levels achieved at the end of the 1970s and during most of the 1980s (Figure 26, second panel). A report by Statistics Canada[40] explains this by the fact that strong investment in machinery and equipment over the past recession and recovery implies an increased need for firms to train labour and therefore a delay in potential productivity gains.

Various studies provide broad support for these interpretations of Canada's aggregate productivity performance; however, they also caution that such per-formance may vary across industries. One of these studies[41] analysed total factor

Table 16. **Productivity growth in the business sector**

Per cent changes at annual rates

	Labour productivity			Total factor productivity		
	1960-73	1973-79	1979-94 [1]	1960-73	1973-79	1979-94 [1]
United States	2.2	0.0	0.8	1.6	−0.4	0.4
Japan	8.3	2.9	2.5	5.6	1.3	1.4
Germany	4.5	3.1	0.9	2.6	1.8	0.5
France	5.3	2.9	2.3	3.7	1.6	1.3
Italy	6.3	2.9	1.8	4.4	2.0	0.9
United Kingdom	3.9	1.5	2.0	2.6	0.6	1.6
Canada	2.9	1.5	1.2	2.0	0.6	−0.1
Big 7	4.3	1.4	1.4	2.9	0.6	0.8

1. 1979-93 for Japan, Germany and Italy.
Source: OECD, *National Accounts*; Secretariat estimates.

productivity growth and trends in relative efficiency levels in the national two-digit manufacturing industries of Canada, the United States and Japan. Viewed broadly, until the mid-1980s the productivity performance of Canadian manufacturing industries was not unequivocally worse than that of the other two countries. However, more recent data suggest that, in the second half of the 1980s, US manufacturers enjoyed higher TFP growth in virtually all industries. It is not clear to what extent the recent rebound in TFP has reversed this trend. OECD Secretariat estimates for labour productivity levels by 3-digit industries show that in the majority of industrial sectors (and on average) Canada's relative position in 1993 was still much less favourable than in 1986. The pervasiveness of the problem is suggestive of more fundamental causes, some of which are examined later in the chapter.

Structural change

A relatively stagnant industrial structure has been considered a major weakness of the Canadian economy. As a result, Canada has retained a relatively large share of its resources in primary industries and has redeployed a comparatively small share into high-technology sectors. This is highlighted by data in Figure 27 which show only a slight decrease in the share of total manufacturing employment in natural resource-based sectors, along with a modest increase in the employment share of science-based industries. At the same time, there was a

Figure 26. **ALTERNATIVE MEASURES OF TOTAL FACTOR PRODUCTIVITY**

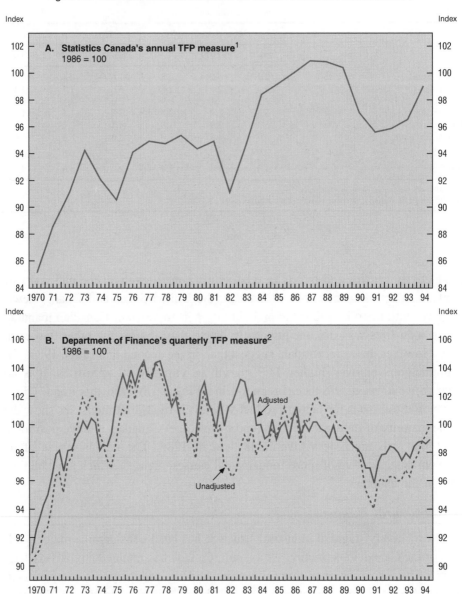

1. Gross multifactor productivity on hours, business sector.
2. Commercial sector.
Source: CANSIM – Statistics Canada; Department of Finance.

Figure 27. **EMPLOYMENT SHARES IN THE MANUFACTURING SECTOR BY TYPE OF INDUSTRY**
Per cent

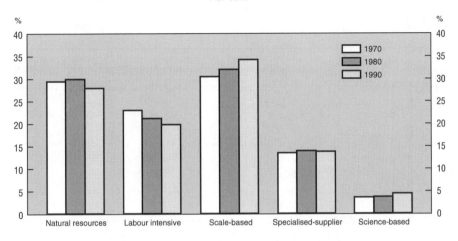

Source: OECD, STAN database.

more prominent fall and rise, respectively, in the share of manufacturing employment in labour-intensive industries and in scale-based industries.

Extensive analysis of structural changes in the Canadian economy was compiled by *The Royal Commission on the Economic Union and Development Prospects* in the mid-1980s. One study done for this Commission identified changes over time in the relative shares of national output, labour and capital inputs accounted for by different sectors of the economy, comparing them with those for other countries.[42] Viewed broadly, the evidence suggested that, through the early 1980s, structural readjustment was occurring as quickly in Canada as in other developed countries with the exception of Japan and West Germany. However, faster readjustments exhibited by the latter two countries were seen to reflect, to some extent, a ''catching-up'' process and therefore to overstate longer-run speeds of structural readjustment in those two economies relative to Canada.

An OECD study[43] examined the extent and direction of structural change in several member countries from the early 1970s through to the mid-1980s, using

Figure 28. **CHANGES IN OUTPUT SHARE
BY LEVEL OF TECHNOLOGY**
Per cent

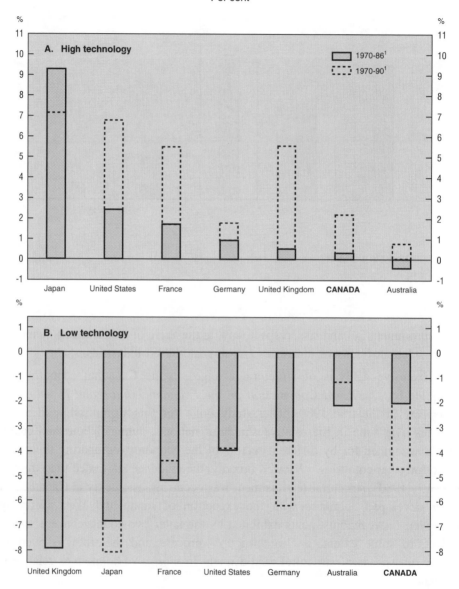

1.   United States from 1972; Germany from 1976.
Source: OECD (1992), STAN database.

80

an input-output decomposition technique. The study found that Canada (and Australia) had relatively small shifts in output shares into high-growth and out of low-growth industries. In particular, Canada was one of the only two countries experiencing gains in medium-technology manufacturing. While in many other countries the output share of high-technology industries increased considerably, in Canada it remained virtually unchanged (Figure 28). An update of these findings suggests that there was some shift towards high-technology industries in the second half of the 1980s, but this trend was even more pronounced in many other OECD countries.

A more recent study[44] extends the OECD analysis for Canada, with a wider coverage and finer industrial disaggregation. Its results broadly support OECD findings. While medium-technology industries boomed in the first half of the 1980s, they have lost ground to high-technology industries since. However, contrary to widely-held perceptions, the speed of change in the Canadian economy does not appear to be rising. As can be seen from the indicators in Table 17, the pace of structural change may have accelerated over the early 1980s, but has certainly not increased, and if anything, has decreased in the late 1980s and early 1990s. To the extent that there has been structural change, however, foreign trade has become its prime catalyst.[45]

Several other recent studies, which evaluate structural change in Canadian industries in the 1980s and early 1990s, also conclude that competition, espe-

Table 17. **The pace of structural change**

Gross output

	Lilien index [1]		Dissimilarity index [2]	
	50 industries	111 industries	50 industries	111 industries
1971-81 [3]	1.93	2.54	1.65	2.06
1981-86 [4]	2.38	3.02	2.05	2.43
1986-91 [5]	1.80	2.27	1.57	1.81

1. The Lilien index is a measure of divergence in the sectors' output growth. It is calculated as the standard deviation of annual output growth weighted by sector output.
2. The dissimilarity index is a measure of divergence in the sectors' output shares. It corresponds to half of the sum of absolute changes in output shares by sector.
3. 1971 prices.
4. 1981 prices.
5. 1986 prices.
Source: Gera and Mang (1995).

cially from the external sector, appears to be an important influence on the nature and extent of recent industrial restructuring.[46] This is consistent with findings that the amount of restructuring has been associated with the labour-intensity of a given industry and the extent of pre-existing tariff barriers in that industry. At the same time, exports have become an increasingly important factor for change in high-technology industries, which have more recently tended to gain in terms of total employment and output compared with labour-intensive sectors.

Foreign trade

As discussed in Chapter I, Canada's external balance has been in sizeable deficit over the past decade or so. While macroeconomic influences and exchange-rate developments have played a role in this regard, one structural factor behind the external deficit is the low share of exports of services by international comparison. Contrary to the service account, merchandise trade has traditionally been in surplus, but the latter has tended to decline in relation to GDP, notwithstanding some widening more recently. Underlying this development has been a marked impact of changes in price competitiveness on export shares while import penetration has displayed a steady upward trend (see Figure 9 in Chapter I). The composition of Canada's merchandise trade partly explains these divergent trends.

As noted earlier, Canada's trade pattern has long been dominated by an export specialisation in resource and scale-intensive industries (see Table 18) where price competitiveness plays a significant role. Non-price factors such as quality and novelty of products, product differentiation and marketing strategies tend to be of secondary importance. As a result, Canada's export performance has been very sensitive to the deterioration in competitiveness that resulted from sluggish productivity growth and exchange-rate appreciation in the second half of the 1980s and the early 1990s. Given the different product mix (Table 15), imports have been less responsive to these influences. Import penetration has increased steadily in areas where non-price factors determine international competitiveness. This is the case of various high-technology sectors (electronics, computers, pharmaceuticals) where Canada is at a comparative disadvantage. As can be seen from Table 18, Canada's import penetration rate in this field is far higher than in other major OECD countries.

Table 18. **Export specialisation and import penetration by type of industry**

Per cent

	Canada		United States		G7[1]	
	1973	1992	1970	1992	1970	1992
	Export specialisation[2]					
High-technology	49	57	167	150	102	102
Medium-technology	120	116	111	90	108	105
Low-technology	99	113	62	74	92	95
High-wage	132	123	136	118	94	89
Medium-wage	92	93	90	95	102	103
Low-wage	78	76	74	82	86	90
Resource-intensive	146	153	77	88	86	88
Labour-intensive	27	33	56	62	102	99
Scale-intensive	143	148	86	82	105	103
Specialised supplier	44	50	124	110	102	101
Science-based	61	55	214	178	103	102
	Import penetration[3]					
High-technology	47.6	71.1	6.6	24.5	19.7	35.9
Medium-technology	44.4	53.9	8.6	21.3	20.8	31.6
Low-technology	13.8	19.8	5.4	9.5	12.5	18.8
High-wage	46.5	54.3	8.6	20.3	19.8	32.9
Medium-wage	27.8	39.8	5.7	13.5	15.0	22.0
Low-wage	14.5	25.1	6.1	15.1	12.5	20.9
Resource-intensive	10.1	15.3	6.2	7.7	11.9	16.4
Labour-intensive	19.4	34.1	5.7	21.4	13.5	27.0
Scale-intensive	38.0	45.9	7.5	15.3	16.3	26.6
Specialised supplier	43.7	62.3	6.8	26.4	18.8	32.2
Science-based	74.3	78.6	5.3	19.5	30.2	43.8

1. Unweighted average.
2. Export specialisation (or revealed comparative advantage) is the ratio of the share of the country's exports in a particular industry in its total manufacturing exports to the share of total OECD exports. A value of 100 indicates the same export specialisation as the OECD average.
3. 1973 for the United States. 1992 figures for Canada and the United States are estimates.
Source: OECD, STAN database.

Figure 29 looks at recent trends in trade specialisation in more detail: the upper right quadrant shows those industries where Canada had a revealed comparative advantage in 1989, that has since increased further (*e.g.* wood products, non-ferrous metals); the upper left quadrant depicts those industries where Canada's export specialisation has intensified, without, as yet, constituting a revealed comparative advantage (*e.g.* electronics, pharmaceuticals). Overall, it

Figure 29. **MANUFACTURING EXPORT SPECIALISATION**[1]

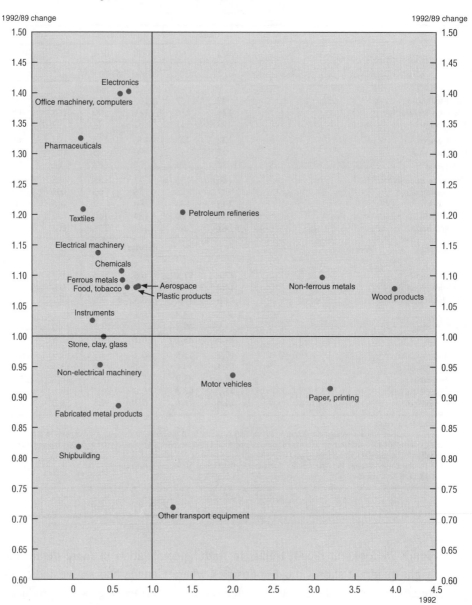

1. Export specialisation (revealed comparative advantage) = [X(j, k)/X(k)]/[X(j, o)/X(o)] where X = exports of country j, total OECD o and industry k.
    Source: OECD Secretariat.

appears that the picture is mixed, with both traditional and knowledge-based sectors gaining ground. The current trade specialisation thus carries future risks. Typically, resource-intensive products are not in growing market segments as primary inputs account for a declining share of inputs in industrial production. Indeed, constant market share analysis shows that product composition has had an adverse effect on Canada's export performance, although this has been partly offset by a favourable country composition of export markets.[47] Moreover, the importance of price competitiveness for resource-intensive products makes Canada's market shares vulnerable to competition from emerging low-cost countries.

Although exports by other industries, including various high-technology sectors, are gradually becoming more important, at the same time, as noted, import penetration rates in these industries are rising strongly. Canada's export/import ratio in "high-tech" products (aerospace, electronic equipment, office machinery and computers and pharmaceuticals) compared with other OECD countries indicates a relative comparative disadvantage in these areas (Table 19). To the extent one subscribes to the view that innovation opportunities are more plentiful in conventionally defined high-technology industries than elsewhere, this suggests the possibility of an "innovation gap" between Canada and other developed countries.

Table 19. **Export/import ratios for high-technology industries**[1]

	Canada	United States	OECD
Aerospace	0.96	3.26	1.45
Electronic equipment	0.45	0.96	1.06
Office machinery and computers	0.46	0.76	0.83
Pharmaceuticals	0.24	1.39	1.18

1. 1992.
Source: OECD, *Main Science and Technology Indicators.*

Impediments to better industrial performance and policy response

A number of factors have been identified that may be impediments to a better industrial performance. They include *i)* an "innovation gap" associated with low, and to a large extent public, expenditure on research and development (R&D) as well as certain attitudes and behaviour that are handicaps to developing a more adaptive and flexible economy; *ii)* weaknesses in Canada's small and medium-sized business organisations, especially in technology-intensive industries; and *iii)* infrastructure deficiencies, especially with respect to "information highway" technology. Progress towards a more efficient industrial framework also calls for further trade liberalisation, although significant achievements have been made in this area in recent years. These issues are addressed in turn as well as the policy initiatives taken in response.

The "innovation gap"

The view is widely held that Canadian industry suffers from an "innovation gap" compared with other developed countries. Indeed, various issues of the *World Competitiveness Report* rank Canada poorly on entrepreneurial drive and R&D activities,[48] although the country's relative position has tended to improve more recently. In the paragraphs below, factors potentially contributing to this alleged technological gap and organisational rigidities are addressed. They relate to limited activity in the field of science and technology, reflecting insufficient efforts in research and development, as well as to private and public sector attitudes that have contributed to an inflexible and non-innovative industrial structure.

Limited scientific and technological activity

More direct measures of scientific and technological activity show Canada in an unfavourable light in any international comparison. In particular, in the number of domestic patents granted to residents per head of population, the number of those patents filed within the country as well as the number of scientists and engineers per person in the labour force, Canada has consistently some of the lowest ratios among industrialised countries. Moreover, compared to their global competitors, Canadian firms rank last in company-funded R&D, with only a tiny fraction (less than 1 per cent) undertaking any R&D at all[49] (see below). However, while Canadian residents account for only a handful of world total patents in any year, which places them far behind Japanese and Americans, there is no indication that Canada's relative performance in this area deteriorated

86

over time. Also, Canada has apparently been as quick to move out of "stagnant" patenting sectors and into 'active' ones as other OECD countries.[50]

Some critics have argued that input measures such as R&D expenditures, and even output measures such as patents, may not be reliable indicators of innovation activity in Canadian industries. In particular, the transfer of technology within foreign multinational enterprises to their Canadian affiliates implies that Canada may have access to new technology without having to spend proportionally as much on R&D and related activities as its trading partners, given the relatively high foreign ownership levels in Canadian industry. Thus, the speed and extent of commercial utilisation of new technology might be more important than its generation insofar as the productivity and competitiveness of Canadian industries are concerned.

Various studies have examined the rates of adoption of new technology in Canada compared with other countries.[51] In individual cases, Canadian organisations have proved to be slower than their US counterparts to introduce new technology. In other cases, no significant differences in adoption patterns can be identified. Moreover, adjusting for differences in the size distribution of firms reduces the observed diffusion gap for Canada in certain cases. An implication of the diffusion evidence is that R&D and patenting data may overstate the magnitude of any innovation gap between Canada and other developed countries.

Insufficient R&D efforts

- R&D expenditure: size and funding

Canada's R&D expenditure as a share of GDP is among the lowest in the OECD area, both in the private sector and overall (Figure 30). Although the R&D expenditure-to-GDP ratio has increased, amounting to 1½ per cent in recent years, Canada's relative position has remained unchanged (Table 20). The business sector performs just over half of total R&D compared with over two-thirds OECD-wide. This reflects an investment gap on the industry side rather than any "over-investment" by the government compared with other OECD countries.

Within the public sector, the federal government accounts for about one-third of the R&D effort, the rest being carried out by higher educational institutions and non-profit laboratories. The federal government is also an active direct and indirect funder of R&D. Specifically, it finances almost 30 per cent of the R&D undertaken in Canada, and indirectly an additional share of 10 per cent

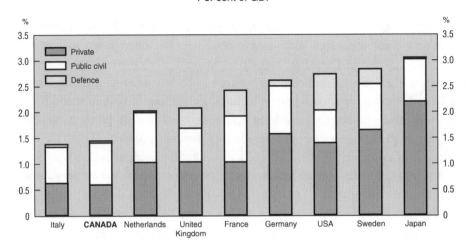

Figure 30. **INTERNATIONAL COMPARISON OF R&D EXPENDITURE**[1]
Per cent of GDP

1. 1991. Netherlands 1990, Sweden 1989.
Source: OECD, *Basic Science and Technology Statistics.*

through its funding (with the provinces) of higher education (Table 21). As is the
case for the carrying out of R&D, this is also more than on average in the OECD.
However, it is worth noting that the share of government-financed R&D expenditure of businesses is lower in Canada than in the other OECD countries.

Table 20. **R&D expenditure by sector of performance**

Percentages

	Total[1]		Business sector[2]		Government[2]		Higher education[2]		Private non-profit[2]	
	1981	1993	1981	1993	1981	1993	1981	1993	1981	1993
Canada	1.2	1.5	48.7	54.4	23.4	17.9	27.0	26.4	0.8	1.3
France	2.0	2.4	58.9	62.1	23.6	20.1	16.4	16.4	1.1	1.4
Germany	2.4	2.5	70.2	66.9	13.7	15.2	15.6	17.5	0.5	0.4
Japan	2.1	2.9	66.0	71.1	12.0	10.0	17.6	14.0	4.5	4.9
United Kingdom	2.4	2.2	63.0	65.9	20.6	13.8	13.6	16.5	2.8	3.8
United States	2.4	2.7	70.8	71.8	12.1	10.0	14.5	14.8	3.1	3.4
Total OECD	2.0	2.3	65.8	67.4	15.0	12.7	16.6	17.1	2.6	2.9

1. Per cent of GDP.
2. Per cent of total.
Source: OECD, STIU databases.

Table 21. **Performance and funding of R&D**

Percentage of total

	1971-75	1976-80	1981-85	1986-90	1991-93
Performing sector					
Federal government	29	24	20	16	15
Higher education	31	30	26	25	26
Business enterprise	35	41	50	55	54
Funding sector					
Federal government	43	36	34	30	28
Higher education	15	16	12	10	10
Business enterprise	29	35	38	42	42

Source: Statistics Canada.

Not only is business spending on R&D low, but also very few Canadian companies carry out formal R&D activities. As a result, industrial R&D expenditures are highly concentrated among a small number of companies. In 1993, the 50 largest R&D performers in Canada accounted for almost 60 per cent of all industrial R&D expenditure, and the top 25 performers for almost 50 per cent (Table 22). While concentration of R&D spending declined slightly over the period 1973 to 1993, it remains that a handful of companies do a disproportionate share of R&D.

As noted, one possible factor explaining modest R&D efforts is the high level of foreign ownership. Foreign sources account for a much higher share of R&D financing than in most other OECD countries (18 per cent compared with

Table 22.   **Concentration of industrial R&D among Canadian companies**

Percentage of R&D expenditures

	Top 10	Top 25	Top 50
1973	35	51	64
1979	38	54	62
1983	37	52	63
1989	35	49	59
1993	37	49	59

Source: Statistics Canada.

2½ per cent OECD-wide). Still, it is likely that R&D tends to be carried out in national headquarters, adversely affecting measures of R&D intensity in Canada. Indeed, across industries, foreign affiliates' R&D intensity is in most cases lower than that of domestic firms (Table 23). This is likely to affect aggregate R&D intensity significantly, as foreign affiliates are most present in high and medium-technology branches where large amounts of R&D are carried out. Low R&D intensity in these sectors does not, however, necessarily imply that technology transfers do not take place from headquarters to subsidiaries since these can

Table 23. **R&D and sales of foreign affiliates and domestic firms**

Selected industries, 1990

	Share of foreign affiliates		R&D intensity [1] of		Relative R&D intensity [2]
	In industry sales	In industry R&D expenditure	Foreign affiliates	Domestic firms	
Cars, parts, accessories	91.1	59.0	0.2	1.4	0.65
Rubber products	90.9	75.0	0.3	1.0	0.83
Office machines, computers	87.8	74.0	3.0	7.5	0.84
Pharmaceuticals and medicine	87.5	84.0	4.6	6.0	0.96
Other chemical products	87.0	87.0	1.4	1.4	1.00
Other electrical products	79.4	61.0	0.9	2.2	0.77
Wholesale trade	73.7	64.0	1.2	1.9	0.87
Fabricated metal products	69.4	44.0	0.8	2.3	0.63
Non-metallic mineral products	62.5	67.0	0.6	0.5	1.07
Other electronic equipment	60.6	47.0	9.7	16.5	0.78
Scientific, professionnal equipment	59.6	27.0	1.2	4.8	0.45
Textiles	59.3	86.0	1.7	0.6	1.45
Machinery	46.2	27.0	1.8	4.1	0.58
Construction	42.4	9.0	0.4	2.9	0.21
Primary industries	41.7	29.0	0.4	0.7	0.70
Primary metals (non-ferrous)	34.4	48.0	1.6	0.9	1.40
Electronic parts and components	30.6	13.0	3.3	9.7	0.42
Food	28.0	66.0	0.5	0.1	2.35
Paper and allied products	22.4	7.0	0.1	0.4	0.31
Other manufactured industries	21.5	4.0	0.7	4.5	0.19
Plastic products	13.8	8.0	1.1	2.0	0.58
Engineering and scientific services	11.2	28.0	41.7	13.5	2.50
Computer and rel. services	10.7	5.0	7.5	15.6	0.47
Finance, insurance, real estate	6.4	5.0	0.4	0.5	0.78

1. R&D expenditure as a percentage of sales.
2. R&D intensity of foreign affiliates/R&D intensity of firms.
Source: OECD, Foreign Affiliates Database.

either take the form of embodied R&D or direct transfer of knowledge (for example, through licences and patents).

Another way of assessing a country's technological competitiveness is the calculation of a "modified R&D intensity", which indicates what the R&D performance would be for a country if its economic structure was identical to the average of all countries in the analysis.[52] As was to be expected, this indicator raises Canada's R&D intensity (Figure 31). But structural disadvantages do not entirely explain Canada's "innovation gap". Even with an "average" industrial structure, the R&D intensity in Canadian manufacturing would be only half that of the leading country.[53]

Would Canadian organisations be more innovative and flexible if they performed more R&D, both absolutely and relatively to foreign competitors? Would the innovation benefits of R&D be higher if government performed and funded less while industry did more? Available research on the consequences and determinants of industrial R&D offer some insights into these issues.

Figure 31. **R&D INTENSITY IN MANUFACTURING**[1]
Percentages

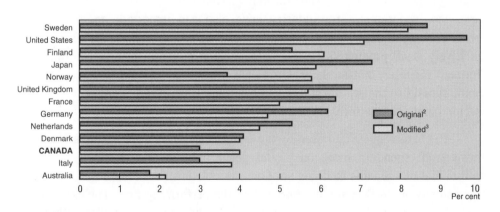

1. 1990 data. 1989 data for Norway, Canada and Australia.
2. R&D expenditure relative to value added.
3. Sum of the R&D intensity for each sector of a country weighted by the average value added share of the sector in 13 OECD countries.
Source: OECD, STAN/ANBERD database.

- Effects and determinants of R&D

A wide range of studies for both the United States and Canada identify a positive and strong relationship between productivity growth rates (either total or partial productivity) and the accumulation of R&D capital.[54] On balance, R&D investment in Canada is estimated to account for anywhere between 20 and 60 per cent of the proportion of productivity growth experienced. However, this does not necessarily imply that Canada is "underspending" significantly on R&D. The returns-to-R&D experienced to date presumably reflect the selection of projects with the most attractive prospects. On the other hand, the underlying technological opportunities facing Canada and other countries appear to be expanding given the accelerating pace of technological change in activities such as microelectronics, telecommunications, biotechnology, materials and materials-handling and so forth. These latter developments would presumably increase the potential marginal rates of return to commercially oriented R&D.[55]

While exceptions can be found for specific activities, the general conclusion of available studies is that government-performed and funded R&D has smaller productivity-enhancing effects than privately conducted R&D.[56] However, most of the available studies focus on the United States where government financing of R&D is concentrated on military technology with limited commercial applications. In fact, as will be discussed below, Canadian government technological assistance programmes for industry have also had important non-commercial objectives, most notably the promotion of regional development. As a result, relatively small productivity effects of Canadian government-financed (and performed) R&D are not unlikely. On balance, therefore, available research lends some support to the argument that Canadian industry would benefit if the private sector spent (and performed) more on R&D.

An obvious question raised by the analysis above is what restrains Canadian firms from spending more on – and performing more – R&D if there are substantial net benefits to doing so. One possible answer is that a large share of the benefits of R&D is not appropriated by the performing firm. The existence of large R&D externalities (or spillovers) indeed results in a potentially inefficiently low level of private spending on R&D from a society-wide perspective.[57] This, in turn, implies a need for public policies designed to stimulate increased R&D spending and performance by the private sector. Grants and tax incentives have been the main financial approaches taken by government to achieve this objective (see below).

There has been relatively little critical analysis of how effective these incentives are at stimulating net increases in private sector R&D.[58] Major concerns about grants are that recipients will be selected, at least in part, for non-economic reasons, and that, on balance, they may not lead to additional R&D, but rather encourage firms to substitute public for private funding. In fact, the available evidence suggests that for Canadian-owned firms, at least, government grants do lead to increased R&D spending by the grant recipient, although statistically significant increases are identifiable only for specific industries, such as electrical equipment manufacturers.

By their nature, tax credits do not discriminate among firms undertaking the type of activity covered by the tax legislation. To that extent, this instrument is less susceptible to political influence than is the distribution of grants. A recognised shortcoming of tax credits is that they are of little use to start-up firms and others that are not making profits (and paying taxes) unless the credits are refundable, can be carried forward for long periods of time or sold to companies in a position to make use of them. Another potential drawback is that more firms may be eligible for the tax credit than are capable of carrying out the type of R&D that generates significant spillover productivity benefits for the economy. (The Scientific Research and Development Tax Credit discussed in the next section may be illustrative of this latter concern.) The impact of tax credits on private funding of R&D has also been found to be positive, although the magnitude of the effect is open to question.

In *summary*, there is some empirical justification for arguments that Canada's performance as an industrial innovator would be enhanced if Canadian firms undertook absolutely and relatively more R&D. Moreover, the emphasis should be on privately-financed and performed R&D. Both theory and evidence are more equivocal concerning the "optimal" way for government to encourage increased commercially-oriented R&D. However, the fact that until recently 41 different federal government departments spent money on R&D suggests a potential for increased efficiency in administration, better harmonisation of objectives and gathering of underlying economies of scale and scope.[59]

Public and private sector attitudes

Attitudes of both the public and private sectors are important in the development of a flexible and innovative industrial structure. Historically, Canadian governments have been hesitant to embrace market competition across a wide range of activities and/or as being inclined to protect domestic economic interests (either at a national or provincial level) at the expense of consumers and at the cost of lower economic efficiency. An orientation toward basic factor advantages has allegedly led many Canadian-based firms in resource industries to pursue cost-based strategies premised on static views of cost determination, rather than investing in new technologies in order to improve their cost positions. In non-resource industries, relatively high barriers to trade have, in the past, encouraged Canadian firms to proliferate products uneconomically, rely unduly upon domestic sources of product and diversify widely. Most industries that do export, particularly outside the resource sector, are oriented primarily to the United States as a stepping stone to broader global markets. As a result, many Canadian firms allegedly do not reap the benefits that flow from being integrated into international markets for goods and technology and from being exposed to a wide range of extremely demanding buyers.[60]

It is not possible in this chapter to present the substantial amount of research that has been done on these issues. It might be noted that the evidence is overwhelmingly in support of the hypothesis that reducing barriers to competition – whether originally erected against foreign rivals or against potential domestic rivals – leads to improved efficiency and heightened responsiveness to market developments. For example, reductions in tariff and non-tariff barriers have been found to lead to strong gains in productivity and to stimulate a faster rate of adoption of new technology.[61] There is evidence that increased inward foreign direct investment confers spillover productivity benefits upon domestically-owned firms, primarily through increased competitive pressure.[62] Deregulation of domestic industries such as transportation and telecommunications has been found to contribute to lower unit costs as more efficient combinations of factor inputs and production techniques are employed.[63] There is no consistent evidence, however, that public enterprises are inherently less efficient than private firms,[64] although privatisation can be expected to contribute to increased efficiency to the extent that it is accompanied by policies promoting increased competition.

In short, there is now a broad recognition in Canada that promoting increased competition wherever possible is an effective way to encourage innovation and organisational flexibility among domestic firms. Indeed, exposure to global competition can be seen as the linchpin of any set of policies designed to restructure domestic industries in the direction of being more innovative, flexible and responsive to consumers. Canadian firms recognised this trend in the late 1970s and embraced a comprehensive approach to the Tokyo Round of trade negotiations. In the early 1980s, they reversed a historical position of protection of Canadian industry from US competition by advocating a bilateral free trade agreement to force the pace of adjustment in the Canadian economy. In fact, as will be discussed in a later section, Canadian government policies over the late 1980s and early 1990s did embrace increased competition as an instrument of industrial restructuring, in particular by implementing the Free Trade Agreement with the United States, the NAFTA, and the Uruguay Round. Furthermore, government policy also moved significantly towards deregulation and privatisation. Canadian industry responded by undertaking significant restructuring in the late 1980s and early 1990s, some five years behind the United States. As will be described further below, the federal government is currently intensifying its effort to encourage restructuring and competitiveness by adopting a comprehensive microeconomic policy framework. The following paragraphs concentrate on policy initiatives which have aimed at fostering scientific and technological activity.

Policy initiatives to promote science and technology

As noted above, tax credits and grants have been the main instruments to encourage spending on R&D. In fact, tax incentives for private sector R&D are relatively generous in Canada compared with other countries.[65] Grants have been somewhat less important but still substantial. During the 1980s, there was some attempt made by the federal government to consolidate its grant programmes to promote R&D and innovation. Yet, tangible benefits of such programmes – at both the federal and provincial government levels – have been difficult to identify, possibly because until the early 1990s science and technology initiatives remained partly bound up with regional development motives.[66] Furthermore, efforts to ''streamline'' the proliferation of individual programmes had not gone as far as might be desirable.

The Government's recent industrial strategy document[67] did not announce any specific initiatives in the area of science and technology but indicated that a soon-to-be completed Science and Technology Review would put forward recommendations to ensure that, as the largest single investor in science and technology in Canada, the federal government plays an effective role in developing and getting to market commercial products and services.

The federal government's major R&D support programme, the Scientific Research and Experimental Development tax incentive, came under review in the last Budget. One change is that banks and other financial institutions will not be able to collect federal research and development tax credits pending a government review of the entire programme. A major concern is the claiming of tax credits for upgrades to computer software and hardware, including customising off-the-shelf software programmes. This latter practice is seen as being inconsistent with the basic objective of the programme: to develop ''cutting-edge'' technology. Circumscribing claims under the Scientific Research and Experimental Development tax incentive programme is also motivated by a concern about the exploding value of foregone tax revenues associated with use of the programme.

Moreover, as discussed in Chapter II, the last Budget evidenced a concern about federal government deficits by slashing subsidies to business by nearly C\$2.3 billion over the period 1995/96 to 1998/99. Industry Canada will wind down all but 11 of its 54 subsidy and support programmes by the fiscal year 1997/98. Its budget will decline by C\$ 0.5 billion over this period, a cut of over 40 per cent. Furthermore, regional development programmes will see their funding decline to C\$0.6 billion in 1997/98 from C\$1.4 billion in 1994/95. However, given the Government's commitment to science and technology support, expenditure cuts in this area are relatively limited.

Weaknesses of small and medium-sized enterprises

The policy focus on the small and medium-sized enterprises (SME) sector is motivated by the view that it is the most dynamic, competitive and productive sector of the economy. Evidence from the United States suggests that small firms, on average, contribute more innovations per employee than do large firms. In addition, the growing prominence of small firms tends to increase the ''responsiveness'' of the economy. In particular, smaller enterprises tend to achieve greater flexibility through a greater reliance on variable factors of production. Also, because of their simpler organisational structures, smaller enterprises may be better able than their larger counterparts to pursue strategies emphasising flexible corporate and business-level strategies.[68]

Concerns about Canadian SMEs

Concern about SMEs in Canada[69] is related both to the minimal amount of R&D they perform and their weak participation in export markets. For example, of the approximately 900 000 Canadian businesses, only 8 per cent exported in 1992 (just over 15 per cent if manufactures alone are considered). At the same time, Canada's 100 largest exporters accounted for more than 60 per cent of total Canadian exports.[70] It should be noted that data reporting direct exports by size class of firm may give an unduly pessimistic assessment of the export capacity of SMEs to the extent that they supply larger firms that are export intensive. However, it is unlikely that accounting for indirect exports would reverse the conclusion that Canadian SMEs tend to be largely domestically-oriented both absolutely and relatively to their US counterparts.[71] While it is also possible that conventional R&D statistics understate the innovation activities of SMEs, they point to minimal R&D efforts. For example, only 0.4 per cent of Canadian firms (fewer than 3 600) undertook any R&D in 1991.[72] Canadian SMEs also appear to be laggards in adopting new technology, at least compared with their US counterparts.[73]

A recent survey of Canadian firms[74] found also that the use of advanced technology increases with the size of the company. Large establishments (more than 500 employees) are three times as likely to adopt more than five advanced technologies than the smallest ones (fewer than 20 employees). Only large firms combine technologies from different areas (design and engineering, fabrication and assembly, inspection and communications, manufacturing information systems and integration and control) to any extent. Lower rates of R&D spending and technology adoption in small firms could thus form another partial explanation for sluggish aggregate productivity performance. However, these findings must be set against evidence that successful small firms are innovative in ways that differ from formal research or technology use, in particular organisational flexibility, orientation towards customers, product quality and employee skills.[75] Rather than R&D activity and patents, the most important sources of innovation for small firms are customers, suppliers and competitors. In sum, the issue behind innovation in the SME sector is much less firm size as such than a comparatively low share of small businesses that grow and innovate successfully.

Several factors have been hypothesised as contributing to the apparent lack of dynamism in Canada's SME sector. One suggestion is that smaller firms face higher costs of debt capital than their larger counterparts, although there is no evidence of a systematic disadvantage in this respect. Furthermore, a concentration of venture capital funding among a limited number of industries is seen to put SMEs at a disadvantage in capital markets, while high government debt and taxes[76] tend to further exacerbate difficulties in financing small businesses externally or through retained earnings.[77] Moreover, government financing of R&D does not especially favour smaller firms, as is suggested by the evidence presented in Table 24. Specifically, the share of federal and provincial government funding of R&D programmes tends to rise fairly consistently as the R&D size groups increase.

The importance of financing considerations with respect to the performance of Canadian SMEs is unclear, however, and Industry Canada is in the process of commissioning research on this issue. According to business surveys, small enterprises continue to feel that the availability of financing remains a major issue and that banks are not responsive to their needs. Although such funding problems are difficult to quantify,[78] banks have begun to react to this concern with special initiatives aimed at solving them. In addition, as noted above,

Table 24. **Sources of funds for R&D by size of programme**

1991, percentage

R&D size	Performing company	Federal government	Provincial government	Other Canadian sources	Foreign sources
< C$50 000	82	7	2	6	3
50 000-99 999	83	8	2	5	1
100 000-199 999	80	9	2	7	2
200 000-399 999	78	9	3	8	2
400 000-999 999	72	11	3	9	5
> C$999 999	62	7	2	8	20
Total	64	8	2	8	18

Source :   Statistics Canada.

Canada offers generous tax provisions for R&D at both the federal and provincial levels. Nonetheless, such incentives are attractive only insofar as they really lead to tax relief.[79] At the same time, the complexity of the tax system and administrative burdens associated with complying with regulations may be a particularly heavy burden upon the survival and growth of SMEs.[80]

Another argument is that Canadian SMEs suffer from a shortage of expertise in areas of innovation and international business. There is some indirect evidence supporting this argument. For example, a recent survey of Canadian firms has found that more innovative SMEs generally employ a higher percentage of professional and technical/production workers and a lower proportion of other workers than do other firms; in turn, a greater share of these employees are trained.[81] While expertise can often be rented or otherwise acquired from sources such as banks, accounting and management consulting firms and the like, the long-run benefits are arguably likely to be most compelling when it is internal to the organisation. However, small firms rarely have the necessary resources that would provide such expertise internally.

Certainly, small businesses in Canada have been more successful than large firms at creating new jobs[82] over the past decade (Figure 32). However, it is also true that new small businesses have relatively low survival rates. Innovation and accessing export markets appear to be critical factors conditioning the likely long-run success of SME start-ups.[83] Indeed, the few active innovators and exporters among SMEs seem to have made a disproportionate contribution to job creation (well over one-half according to some estimates). The sheer number of SMEs and their relatively large share of total employment in Canada therefore suggest that the country's economic performance might be dramatically improved if this sector became more innovative and export-oriented.

Government support to SMEs

Help to small businesses announced in the Government's industrial strategy document[84] involves reducing regulatory and related burdens as well as increasing their financing capabilities. Regulatory reforms include legislation to simplify and speed up the regulatory process, operational changes that make it easier for businesses to understand regulations, and a requirement that, when they introduce major regulatory changes, federal departments evaluate their impact on business. Specific initiatives to improve the financing capabilities of small businesses

Figure 32. **DISTRIBUTION OF EMPLOYMENT BY SIZE OF BUSINESS**[1]

Per cent

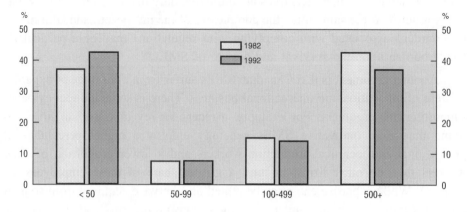

1. Includes self-employed but excludes public administration.
Source: Based on estimates prepared by Entrepreneurship and Small Business Office, Industry Canada, Ottawa.

comprise procurement of goods and services by the federal government,[85] increases in the lending ceiling under the Small Business Loan Act, and commencement of a pilot project to reduce the costs of matching informal investors and other local sources of venture capital with local firms looking for small amounts of equity.

The 1995 federal Budget reinforces the thrust of the policy recommendations in the strategy document. It calls for regional development agencies to provide strategic information to companies (primarily SMEs) in order to help in the development of products and the penetration of export markets. The Government has also taken specific action to target direct export market assistance to meet the needs of SMEs and to ensure that they have an access to export financing similar to that long enjoyed by larger firms. Furthermore, where financial assistance is made available, it will be geared to SMEs and consist primarily of repayable loans rather than grants. The federal government also intends to stimulate commercial bank lending to small businesses by working with the banks to establish performance benchmarks for small business financing against which commercial bank lending behaviour will be evaluated. Finally, the authorities are working to develop a more integrated government-wide SME policy agenda which will focus on further measures to reduce barriers to SME growth (notably in the areas of financing, taxation, technology and innovation).

Infrastructure problems

The potential for increased investment in public sector infrastructure to improve productivity in the private sector has recently become more prominent in Canada with the Government's electoral commitment to renew the country's infrastructure and the emergence of media attention on the "information highway". Politicians and policy makers alike are focusing on information highway investments as a major new source of renewed productivity and economic growth, and the public sector is being urged to play a major role in this field in terms of both hardware and software infrastructure,[86] although the Government considers that the "information highway" should be built, and in large measure financed, by the private sector (see below).

Available evidence on the private sector productivity impact of public sector infrastructure investments is equivocal. Several studies for the United States conclude that there are no productivity benefits in excess of the direct amenities provided by those investments – that is, there are no significant linkages between public sector physical capital and private production activities to support a conclusion that investments in physical infrastructure will contribute to improvements in private sector productivity.[87] There is, however, no unanimity in this respect.[88]

The evidence for Canada is also uncertain. Some econometric studies report that Canadian investment in public infrastructure is a positive and highly significant determinant of variations in Canadian private sector productivity growth.[89] On the other hand, a recent Canadian study,[90] using the growth accounting methodology, concludes that the contribution of public infrastructure investment is of some significance, but not of large importance. The sharp difference in results has been attributed to the fact that, unlike the econometric approach, growth accounting cannot measure the positive "spillovers" of public infrastructure on private sector efficiency.

In any case, the findings of macro studies can provide only a general indication about the relationship between infrastructure and productivity. The rationale for individual projects must be based on rigorous analysis of their likely costs and benefits. With regard to government investments in "information highway" infrastructure, some have argued that government subsidies may have social costs that exceed related benefits.[91] Other reports, however, suggest that there are large social benefits from such investments. Moreover, there appears to be no clear evidence that companies are restricted by available communications technology in implementing new production and management techniques, although the existence of monopoly provision of telecommunication services may have had negative effects on the development of services and technologies.

The authorities have announced a series of initiatives in the field of infrastructure. In particular, the government intends to improve the efficiency of Canada's transportation network by removing or revising outmoded regulations and reducing or eliminating subsidies. It is also privatising or commercialising certain operations. The most notable effort in this regard involves the federal government's sale of its sole ownership of Canadian National Railways. The government also plans to sell off Transport Canada's air navigation system to a new non-government agency, while taking a detailed look at the marine sector, reviewing the operation of the St. Lawrence Seaway, ferry subsidies, ports management and the coastguard. In addition, the Canada Infrastructure Works programme involves a C$ 6 billion partnership of three levels of government to build roads, streets, water treatment facilities, public buildings, parks and so forth.

The country's communication infrastructure is, at the same time, being addressed by specific measures. With substantial investment by the private sector and other levels of government, the federal government will be a partner in creating two segments of the information highway. Increased funding will be provided for the *Canadian Network for the Advancement of Research, Industry and Education* (CANARIE) which is charged with, among other things, creating a high speed experimental communications network and helping innovative companies get more products, services and content on the information highway. The government will also invest in the *SchoolNet* and *Community Access* programmes, respectively designed to link all schools and libraries, and a thousand rural communities to the information highway by 1998. Non-financial initiatives include regulatory reforms in telephony and broadcasting to promote efficiency and innovation through increased competition.[92]

Trade issues

Major initiatives have been taken in the area of international trade in recent years with the Canada-US Free Trade Agreement (FTA) implemented in 1989, and the North American Free Trade Agreement (NAFTA), which includes Mexico, replacing the FTA in 1994.[93] The fundamental relevance of the FTA to Canada remains unchanged under the NAFTA: free trade between Canada and the United States. This has long been identified as offering great prospects for improving the productivity of Canadian industries, in part by stimulating increased competition in Canada. On the other hand, the anticipated impacts of adding Mexico to the free trade area were seen as being relatively limited for Canada.

The primary mechanism by which trade liberalisation was expected to improve industrial productivity in Canada was increased specialisation through stronger intra-industry trade. Hence, changes in trade flows associated with the FTA provide a basis for evaluating the impacts of external trade liberalisation on domestic industrial restructuring. The results of one study,[94] which offers such an assessment based on the period 1989-91, are summarised in Table 25. They clearly show that both merchandise exports and imports between Canada and the United States increased substantially in industries where trade was liberalised under the FTA, whereas they declined in the case of industries unaffected by the FTA. This suggests that sharp increases in intra-industry trade have indeed taken place under the FTA (and the NAFTA), which can be expected to promote improved efficiency among the domestic firms affected. Another finding of the study is that, under the FTA, non-resource-based exports to the United States showed above-average growth, due in large part to the favourable performance of high-technology industries. On the other hand, traditional manufacturing areas had to face a surge of imports from the United States, which contributed to the need for restructuring in these sectors.

The FTA also further liberalised the environment for bilateral direct investment between Canada and the United States, primarily by implementing a provision for national treatment of investment from either member country. However, some sectors are exempt from this provision such as social services, facilities-based communications, cultural industries (including broadcasting) and transportation. The main exemptions under the FTA were carried forward in the NAFTA. It might therefore be argued that the FTA largely left the bilateral direct invest-

Table 25. **Impact of the Free Trade Agreement**
1989-1991

	Exports			
	Value in 1991 (C$ billion)	Per cent exported to the United States	Percentage change in exports to the United States	Percentage change in exports to others
Liberalised				
Resource-based	41 883	61	7.4	−6.5
Non resource-based	19 567	79	34.1	−5.5
Total	61 449	67	16.2	−6.3
Not liberalised				
Total	37 106	63	−2.2	−1.8
	Imports			
	Value in 1991 (C$ billion)	Per cent imported from the United States	Percentage change in imports from the United States	Percentage change in imports from others
Liberalised				
Total	79 769	62	14.0	2.8
Not liberalised				
Total	14 594	70	−8.2	−4.4

Source: Schwanen (1992).

ment environment unaffected. In particular, restrictions in the non-exempt areas were quite limited prior to the Agreement's implementation, while the major sectors in which foreign ownership was relatively low continued to be protected as exempt areas. In fact, there was a sharp increase in Canadian foreign direct investment inflows and outflows in the second half of the 1980s and into the 1990s. However, the US share of Canadian direct investment abroad declined significantly from its peak of 68½ per cent in 1980 to 58 per cent in 1992. At the same time, the US share of foreign controlled assets in Canada decreased from 64 per cent in 1988 to 59 per cent in 1992. Arguably, the imperative for European and Japanese firms to place affiliates inside the North American free trade area accounts for some of the relative increase in the share of non-US direct investment in Canada.

The available evidence suggests that both inward and outward foreign direct investment contributes to industrial restructuring. Inward direct investment generates increased competitive pressures on home country firms and promotes technological change through productivity spillovers. Outward direct investment induces increased specialisation along lines of comparative advantage and also encourages technological change among home country multi-national enterprises by leading them to do more R&D and to "import" state-of-the-art technology.[95] Hence, the potential benefits of further liberalisation in this area are evident.

On the other hand, it is too early to assess the impact of Canada's ratification of the recently concluded Uruguay Round (see Chapter III). Nevertheless, the reductions in trade barriers on labour-intensive goods can be expected to promote further restructuring in those industries, in addition to the adjustments which have been induced by increased international competition since the late 1980s. The somewhat improved economic performance of high-technology industries is also consistent with the finding that the FTA has been associated with increased value-added processing in Canada.

Expanding international trade[96] is seen by the Government as an important means to make the economy more innovative and productive. A strategic emphasis is on dynamic developing markets where Canadian firms have been less successful than in North America. Another element of the strategy is to increase the number of exporters. Specific initiatives planned in this area include the reallocation of funding for trade development, with priority given to small businesses as well as industries and geographic markets with the greatest growth opportunities. Particular emphasis will also be placed on tourism and the agri-food sector. By targeting resources where they make a difference, the authorities expect to make export promotion more effective.

In that context, current efforts by the Canadian Government include advancing trade liberalisation in the western hemisphere through an expansion of NAFTA and encouraging the work now under way on a Free Trade Agreement of the Americas. Multilaterally, Canada is actively pursuing new trade and investment links through Asia Pacific Economic Co-operation (APEC). Other initiatives include attaining improved and more transparent international rules governing such practices as foreign direct investment and anti-competitive practices through a variety of fora, including the OECD. Canadian authorities also have placed a high priority on the full and effective implementation of the new World

Trade Organisation (WTO). Moreover, government support for international trade development and promotion is becoming more strategic. The authorities intend to strengthen partnerships and build an international business team on three fronts: within the federal government, with the provinces and with the private sector. As noted, recent initiatives include working with the provinces to ensure export preparedness, launching a series of innovation products to promote SME participation in global markets, expanding export financing initiatives and providing timely, opportunity-specific market intelligence on sectors and markets that offer the greatest growth potential.

Assessment of the government industrial strategy and future priorities

In November 1994, the Government of Canada presented in a report entitled *Building a More Innovative Economy (BMIE)* a comprehensive industrial strategy designed to increase Canada's international competitiveness so that the private sector can create jobs and raise the standard of living of Canadians. The strategy rests on a four-pronged approach which focuses on promoting a healthy marketplace, strengthening Canada's physical and telecommunications infrastructure, exploiting internal and external trade opportunities, and improving the development and diffusion of technology and innovation throughout the economy (particularly in SMEs). BMIE initiatives involve over fifteen federal departments and agencies and contain more than 55 commitments to action. By this fall, the government will have delivered about 60 per cent of the commitments.

A key feature of the strategy is the development of framework policies and services that secure a competitive marketplace. Canadian authorities indeed consider that having appropriate statutes, regulations and related agencies which define a socially acceptable framework of rights and obligations for the market participants is fundamental to providing a competitive and innovative environment. The strategy thus implies: thoroughly assessing the business impacts of policies, particularly on innovation, investment and trade; setting or adopting international best practices; ensuring horizontal policy co-ordination; and striving for consensus in partnership with all interested parties. The Government's immediate work programme along these lines includes amending such key statutes as the Competition Act, the Bankruptcy and Insolvency Act, the Canada Business

Corporations Act, the Copyright Act, and the Standards Council for Canada Act, amongst others.

Continuation of the privatisation programme, in order to rely more upon competitive market forces, is entirely appropriate to the goal of industrial restructuring, as are continued efforts to streamline the regulatory process to reduce the costs of implementation and compliance. Allowing greater scope for competition in the communications sector is also relevant in this regard, especially given the rising importance of this sector to improving productivity growth in the economy. Streamlining the regulatory process might be of particular benefit to SMEs who have long complained about the particular burdens imposed on them by mandated government paperwork. Recent efforts to mitigate the filing requirements of small businesses under the GST (see Chapter III) are a positive step in this respect.

As there is controversy about the contribution of publicly funded physical infrastructure to private sector productivity, it would seem appropriate for the government to be cautious in financing such investments, especially given the still burdensome public deficit and debt levels. Indeed, the 1995 Budget has reduced considerably, in the near term, federal funding for the Canada Infrastructure Works initiative launched last year. With regard to the "information highway", it would seem advisable that government funding be kept low and provided over a limited period of time, while the authorities concentrate on developing a framework for a fully competitive market structure to ensure maximum efficiency of any such investment. Recent regulatory reforms in telecommunications represent a move in this direction.

Incentives to industrial restructuring through liberalisation of both internal and international trade and investment are supported by the available evidence. As noted in Chapter III, an agreement signed by the federal and provincial governments in July 1994, which became effective in July 1995, made significant progress toward eliminating barriers to the flow of goods, services and labour across provincial boundaries. The importance of reducing remaining trade restrictions among the provinces is underscored by the fact that they trade nearly as much with each other as they do internationally. The expansion of NAFTA to include other countries could be part of any future trade liberalisation efforts, as could negotiations to eliminate long-standing sources of trade friction between Canada and the United States.[97] The government should also give consideration to building upon the direct investment liberalisation provisions under the NAFTA in the context of negotiations in the OECD on a multilateral investment agreement. Furthermore, trade liberalisation under the auspices of the Asia Pacific Economic Co-operation (APEC) would represent a significant potential new stimulus for industrial restructuring in Canada.[98]

Given the overall size and scope of the SME sector, the emphasis by the government on improving the performance of small business in Canada is relevant. It would be clearly desirable to increase the very limited number of small firms which are active exporters and innovators. Official efforts to address any weaknesses in the provision of financial services for small businesses should be complementary to private sector initiatives. The federal government has carried out consultations on whether they will proceed with a procurement programme dedicated to small businesses, with a decision to be announced in the near future. To the extent that continued government deficits are contributing to higher real Canadian interest rates, any benefits of the proposed programme may be mitigated by higher borrowing costs.

More fundamentally, it has been argued that a more appropriate policy initiative would be for the Canadian government to intensify its efforts to persuade the US authorities either to drop their *Buy America* programme or to have Canadian companies designated as being eligible under this programme. The Canadian Government also continues to bar foreign companies from bidding on such items as urban transit equipment, ships, air navigation equipment, Transport Canada purchases and a range of office equipment. Such restrictions on foreign competition reduce pressures on Canadian companies to improve their efficiency. This consideration further underscores the merits of eliminating government purchasing biases within the NAFTA region.

Efforts to liberalise the trade environment for SMEs might be augmented by government assistance to SMEs in the area of export development and promotion. In particular, SMEs might well be at a disadvantage given economies of scale in these activities, as well as the frequent dearth of international marketing and finance expertise resident in these companies. However, it should be ensured that the recently-announced government initiatives will amplify or complement those launched previously, which included proposals to encourage co-operation among small businesses to help achieve the critical size needed to compete in international markets (*The Business Networks Strategy*) and to bring together small firms to design and market globally competitive products (*Canadian Technology Network*).

In addition, the federal government has been criticised for not implementing policies designed to reduce capital costs for SMEs, including increasing the small business income tax deduction and instituting tax incentives for community-sponsored venture capital pools. However, the imperative to reduce government borrowing requirements seems clear and, as noted above, significant improvements in this regard may make it less costly for SMEs to raise capital in domestic financial markets.

Finally, the scaling down of regional development programmes is arguably an appropriate policy to help rationalise the relatively large and fragmented set of government programmes designed to promote innovation and structural readjustment. Such programmes have long been criticised as mixing regional development goals with science and technology objectives, with the result that their effectiveness in stimulating industrial innovation has been mitigated. An overall review of the government's science and technology policy thus seems to be appropriate so as to ensure that programmes of that sort are conducive to innovation in the private sector, especially among SMEs.[99]

Critical to improving innovation will be Canada's ability to harness its science and technology resources to address weaknesses in its economy. Consistent with the necessity to reduce debt, this does not mean increased government spending but rather an approach based on clear priorities, improving efficiency and effectiveness, as well as true partnerships with the private sector and other public sector institutions. Efforts should be made to ensure that Canada's marketplace rules, such as regulations and standards, are competitive internationally. Government financial support for the private sector, when provided, should be investment rather than subsidy based and focused in areas of high growth where spillovers to other firms and industries are large. There is also need to improve the evaluation of government science and technology programmes and to embed these evaluations in the ongoing expenditure planning cycle. Mechanisms need to be put in place to raise awareness of the importance of science and technology generally and to ensure that balanced and well-considered advice to the private sector in this area is a central component of the government's management of the economy.

Overall, the transformation of industrial policy from firm-specific grants to a more broadly-based framework approach, with emphasis on the reduction or removal of structural impediments to growth, is to be welcomed. The fiscal position of the government anyway constrains the use of grants and tax credits as instruments to promote more spending on R&D and other innovation-related activities. At the same time, there does seem to be scope for substantial streamlining of existing government support programmes for business, including those to promote innovation and trade. However, cuts should not be made across the board but be based on a careful evaluation of existing programmes. Initiatives to fund infrastructure projects, including the information highway, should be studied carefully before being undertaken, given the equivocal evidence about their contribution to private-sector productivity growth. Although the government has obviously a role to play in the case of "market failure" (provided that a cost-effective solution is available), further regulatory reform and trade liberalisation, as well as tax reductions as soon as the budget situation allows, would seem to be the most promising ways to improve the competitiveness of Canadian industries.

V. Conclusions

Canada's economic performance further improved in 1994. With real GDP growing by about 4¹/₂ per cent, more economic slack was taken up and unemployment fell to below 10 per cent, while – despite past exchange-rate depreciation – inflation remained under control. At the same time, with gains in competitiveness and strong growth in the United States – Canada's main trading partner – boosting exports, the external current-account deficit narrowed to 2 per cent of GDP by the end of the year, half the rate prevailing in the early 1990s. Moreover, the public-sector deficit has started falling from relatively high levels. Unfortunately, the recovery failed to maintain its momentum in the first half of 1995 as weaker growth in the United States and the slowdown in household demand, in response to earlier rises in interest rates, have led to sluggish activity. As a result, no further inroads have been made recently into unemployment.

The Secretariat projects that, following this "growth pause", the recovery will resume in the second half of 1995, with GDP growth through 1996 again exceeding that of potential output (which is estimated at around 3 per cent per annum). Together with the expected strengthening of activity in the United States, the strong improvement in Canada's international competitive position should allow exports to pick up. In addition, as monetary conditions have eased significantly in recent months, the recovery is expected to become more broadly based, spreading from exports and business investment to private consumption and residential construction. Nevertheless, with continuing – though diminishing – slack in product and labour markets, and on the assumption of a stable exchange rate, inflation is projected to return to the middle of the official target range of 1 to 3 per cent, following some acceleration in the middle of 1995.

There are important risks attached to the short-term outlook, however. One is that, by adversely affecting exports, a "hard landing" of the US economy could imply continued weak activity in Canada. Another is that households may not respond as quickly to interest rate declines as they did to previous increases, either because they prefer to wait for further falls or because they are concerned about employment prospects. Also, despite favourable price performance, financial-market concern about the political situation in Quebec and the high level of Canada's public debt may constrain a further reduction in interest rates which is assumed in the Secretariat projections.

So far, high-risk premia built into Canadian interest rates – which have tended to exceed corresponding US rates by 1 to 2 per cent – have prevented the economy from fully reaping the benefits of a low-inflation environment. Indeed, both price increases and inflation expectations have declined significantly since the introduction of inflation-control targets in 1991. Yet, following some narrowing in differentials, Canadian short and long-term interest rates have tended to rise by more than their US counterparts since early 1994. As the resulting dampening effect on economic activity has not been fully offset by the decline in the Canadian dollar, overall monetary conditions actually tightened. Indeed, the authorities, at times, have had to give precedence to steadying nervous markets, allowing interest rates to rise more than was probably required to hold inflation within the target band.

Short-term interest rates have, however, receded substantially more recently, as the Canadian dollar firmed. Since persistent economic slack, due to the renewed widening in the output gap in the first half of 1995, should continue to put downward pressure on inflation at least through 1996, there may be room for the authorities to allow monetary conditions to ease further in the coming months in the absence of unexpected shocks to demand and inflation. As the output gap narrows progressively, however, vigilance will be required. Indeed, past experience suggests that the consequences of overshooting potential output might prove costly, if inflation targets are to be met. In this regard, some recent initiatives taken by the Bank of Canada to provide more guidance to the market– in particular, the introduction of a target range for the overnight loan rate and the publication of a semi-annual monetary policy report – are to be welcomed, as they should help strengthen the transparency and effectiveness of the Bank's action.

To ease the task of monetary policy and achieve, over time, interest-rate levels consistent with low inflation, additional progress in fiscal consolidation appears essential. The large budget deficits accumulated in the past have been reflected in a rising net public debt-to-GDP ratio, which, at almost 65 per cent of GDP, is now about 25 percentage points higher than in the late 1980s. As a result, net debt interest payments more than account for the government deficit itself. Moreover, an important counterpart of public debt accumulation has been an increase in total net external debt to around 45 per cent of GDP, with related interest payments abroad exceeding the overall current account deficit. Such developments have left the economy vulnerable to financial-market sentiment and explain recent downgrades of sovereign debt by some international credit rating agencies.

The Government which took office in late 1993 has given priority to halting and reversing this long-term deterioration in public finances. With economic growth somewhat stronger than anticipated and actions taken in the 1994 Budget, the federal budget deficit declined by around 1 percentage point to 5 per cent of GDP in the fiscal year 1994/95. The 1995 Budget adopted drastic expenditure reductions in order to ensure both that the further decline in the deficit to just over 4 per cent in fiscal year 1995/96 will be achieved, in spite of higher-than-expected interest rates, and that the 3 per cent interim deficit target for 1996/97 will be met. Measures included significant cuts in federal government pro-grammes, notably subsidies to agriculture and other business, transfers to prov-inces, unemployment insurance as well as a 15 per cent reduction in federal employment.

In the light of recent indicators, there are grounds for optimism that the current deficit target will again be met: indeed, although weaker economic growth is likely to have an adverse effect on government finances, this should be offset by lower interest rates than expected at Budget time. However, this would still imply the persistence of a significant – albeit declining – structural deficit, leaving government finances exposed to a possible economic downturn or interest rate increases. Hence the need for continued fiscal restraint to avoid that progress in reducing the deficit stalls and that the public-debt ratio keeps rising. Since the scope for tax increases appears limited, given the general perception that the tax burden is already too high and the need to maintain competitiveness *vis-à-vis* the United States, further expenditure savings, to keep the growth of spending well below that of GDP, will have to bear the brunt of the adjustment.

Fiscal restraint is also needed at the provincial level, which accounts for about one-third of the general government deficit. Progress in budget consolidation among provinces has been mixed so far. While most provinces either already have achieved budget balance or are planning to do so in the next year or two, the two largest ones – Ontario and Quebec – are lagging behind and still have to take decisive action to curtail expenditure. However, the recently-elected government in Ontario is committed to balance the province's budget by the end of the decade. More generally, there is scope for reforming social programmes administered by the provinces, including health and social assistance, where spending pressures have persisted. In this context, they will have to cope with the reduction in transfers from the federal government which will be implemented in 1996/97 and 1997/98 as part of a wider reform of the federal-provincial transfer system.

The need to generate budget savings together with the concern about identifying impediments to better economic performance has led the government to initiate reviews in several areas of structural policy. A high priority in this regard is the reform of the Unemployment Insurance (UI) system to remove some of the inherent incentive distortions, in particular the tendency of the system to encourage frequent use of the programme and the regional variation in the generosity of benefits which tends to heighten differences in, and overall, unemployment rates. The 1994 Budget already introduced changes to the main parameters of the UI system (reducing the duration of benefits and tightening eligibility criteria), which should ease such distortions. A discussion paper was issued subsequently, outlining options for more radical reform. While the option of differentiating between "frequent users" and other claimants will not be retained, a number of alternative proposals have been discussed, such as extending the period over which average earnings are taken into account for the purpose of benefit calculation and reducing the benefit rate according to previous use. The Government announced in the latest Budget its intention to table overall reform legislation of the UI system in late 1995.

Another pending issue is whether part of the savings from UI reform should be used to expand active labour market programmes or reduce payroll taxes. In comparison with most OECD countries, Canada spends a relatively small share of total labour market expenditure on "active measures" designed to facilitate the reinsertion of the unemployed, and a high share on "passive" income support. However, evaluations of the effectiveness of active measures in the case of Canada have come up with mixed conclusions, depending strongly on the precise design and targeting of the programmes in question. In contrast, the rise

114

in payroll taxes, which has recently been much steeper in Canada than in other major OECD countries, appears to have had significant adverse effects on employment. This would suggest that using any savings from UI reform to increase overall expenditure on active labour market measures should be carefully weighed against the likely gains from lowering payroll taxes or reducing the budget deficit.

Other areas where further structural initiatives would be desirable include public pensions and indirect taxation. Under present arrangements, the ageing of Canada's population would lead progressively to a marked rise in pension expenditure as a proportion of GDP over the next decades, putting potential additional burden on the federal budget. To address this concern, the Government will release later this year a paper on the changes required to ensure the sustainability of the public pension system. Reform to simplify the present indirect tax system also remains a government priority. Proposals to harmonise federal and provincial indirect taxation could lead to substantial gains in economic efficiency as well as lower compliance costs for businesses (especially small ones), which might be further enhanced if the tax base were to be extended as recommended by a recent Parliamentary Committee.

Many of the structural reforms undertaken over the past decade have been motivated by the goal of improving Canada's poor overall productivity performance. Compared with other OECD countries, Canada has had small shifts in output shares from low-growth sectors to high-growth industries. At the same time, economic activity has remained strongly concentrated in natural resources and resource-based primary industries, where Canada undoubtedly has a comparative advantage but which are arguably less prone to technological change. These structural features may help explain why Canadian companies are apparently less innovative than their international competitors, with, as a consequence, relatively slow rates of technological change.

While there has been a shift to high-technology industries more recently, their relative importance in Canada is still much lower than the average of OECD countries. Canada's persistent large trade deficit in "high-tech" products also supports the concern that domestic businesses have not been as innovative and flexible as their international competitors. Data showing that Canadian firms do substantially less research and development than their foreign counterparts further point to an "innovation gap" *vis-à-vis* other developed countries. This does not mean, however, that Canada's innovation performance is necessarily limited by the nature of its industrial structure. There are, in fact, opportunities to be innovative and improve productivity in industries that are not traditionally considered to be technology-intensive. Moreover, the transfer of technology from foreign multinational enterprises established in Canada implies that the country may have access to new technology without having to spend as much as its trading partners, the more so since the foreign ownership level in Canadian industry is relatively high. Nonetheless, taking account of these factors, the balance of evidence still suggests that Canada's innovation performance compares unfavourably with other OECD economies.

The Government has recently outlined a number of proposals to make the economy more innovative and productive. The backdrop to the current industrial strategy is the perception that changes in the wider economic environment – such as the evolution of a globally-integrated economy, increased production capacity of newly-industrialised countries, and a revolution in technology – make it even more important to tackle Canada's "innovation gap". The federal government paper, *Building a More Innovative Economy* provides a broadly-based strategy, linking together many instruments of economic development into a more coherent microeconomic agenda. This strategy focuses on expanding markets through trade, encouraging small business growth, creating a modern infrastructure and promoting science and technology or the application of knowledge through all sectors of the economy.

With the implementation of a Free Trade Agreement with the United States and, subsequently, Mexico (NAFTA), foreign trade has become the prime catalyst of structural changes in the economy and a major factor behind the more recent shift towards "high-tech" industries. Indeed, increased exposure to global competition is seen as the linchpin of the current strategy aimed at making Canadian firms more flexible and innovative. In this respect, the extension of NAFTA to other countries could have positive effects, as could negotiations to eliminate long-standing sources of trade friction between Canada and the United States. The Government should also give consideration to building upon the direct investment liberalisation provisions under NAFTA in the context of discussions in the OECD on a multilateral investment agreement. Trade liberalisation under the auspices of the Asia Pacific Economic Co-operation (APEC) could also represent a significant potential new stimulus for industrial restructuring in Canada.

Given the size of internal trade (which is as large as Canada's international trade), further progress in lowering the remaining inter-provincial barriers could generate additional benefits. The Agreement on Internal Trade, which came into effect in July 1995, represents a positive step in reducing barriers to inter-provincial trade, with specific obligations relating to government procurement, labour mobility and investment. Furthermore, the Agreement sets out the process to include specific provisions on energy and sub-provincial procurement by July 1996 and allows for further liberalisation of internal trade more generally.

Given the overall size and scope of the small business sector, the importance attached by the Government to improving performance in this area is clearly warranted. It is desirable to encourage a greater number of small firms to become active exporters and innovators. Government assistance to export development and promotion would also seem relevant, as small enterprises appear to be rather disadvantaged in this field. Moreover, there is a perception in the private sector that there may be weaknesses in the provision of financial services for small businesses, especially for venture capital, micro loans and lending to knowledge-based firms. The Government should ensure, however, that official efforts to address these weaknesses are complementary to private sector initiatives. Finally, continued efforts to reduce the regulatory and paper burden of the government would be appropriate.

With respect to infrastructure, government financing should be carefully evaluated in the present context of still high government public deficits and debt. Concerning the "information highway", in particular, it would appear advisable that any government funding be kept low and provided over a limited period of time, while the authorities concentrate on developing a competitive market structure in this domain. Finally, it is essential that support programmes on science and technology be conducive to innovation in the private sector, especially among small businesses. For this reason and because the fiscal position constrains the use of grants and tax credits to promote research and development and other innovation-related activities, the recent review and streamlining of government support in this area is to be welcomed. However, any further cuts should not be made across the board but, instead, be based on a thorough evaluation of existing programmes and, wherever possible, innovation assistance be considered in partnership with the private sector on a repayable basis. In this context, the Government intends to release a federal Science and Technology Strategy in the fall of 1995.

In summary, notwithstanding the recent weakening of economic activity, Canada's current economic situation displays a number of favourable elements. With a strongly improved competitive position, the external deficit has narrowed significantly for the first time in a decade. Despite a temporary rise, inflation has remained low, consolidating the gains in competitiveness. Budget deficits have started declining, although further consolidation efforts will be necessary to ensure that the fiscal situation is sustainable. This would strengthen national savings, release resources for domestic investment or foreign debt reduction, and help ease pressures on interest rates, which have held back household demand. Progress in structural reform – notably in the areas of unemployment insurance and taxation – and further comprehensive microeconomic policies to create an innovate business climate would improve prospects for sustained economic growth and job creation.

Notes

1. It should be noted that the growing importance of immigration as a source of population increase may mean that conventional measures of underlying demographic demand are overstated to the extent that immigrants have, at least initially, lower rates of household formation.

2. There is some empirical evidence to suggest that the credibility for a policy of low and stable inflation is rising; see in this respect "Inflation, Learning and Monetary Policy Regimes in the G7 Economies", N. Ricketts and D. Rose, Bank of Canada Discussion paper No. 95-6 and "Changes in the Inflation Process in Canada: Evidence and Implications", D. Hostland, Bank of Canada Discussion paper No. 95-5.

3. Laxton, D., D. Rose and R. Tetlow, "Is the Canadian Phillips Curve Non-Linear?", Bank of Canada, *Working Paper 93-7*. D. Turner, "Speed Limit and Asymmetric Inflation Effects from the Output Gap in the Major Seven Countries", OECD *Economic Studies*, 95/1.

4. Orr, A., M. Edey and M. Kennedy, "The Determinants of Long-Term Interest Rates: 17 Country Pooled-Time-Series Evidence", Economics Department *Working Paper No. 155*, OECD, Paris, 1995.

5. The discussion in this section on "General Government" and later on "The Debt Constraint" makes use of national accounts measures of the deficit and debt as these are more easily internationally comparable. Conversely, the discussion in the sections on the "Federal Government" and "Provincial Government" use public accounts measures of the deficit and debt referring to fiscal years (April to March), since this is the basis on which federal and provincial budgets are formulated. The national accounts measure of the deficit differs from that of the public accounts mainly because the former treats expenditure and revenues on an accrual basis, defines capital transactions relating to existing assets as a financing item, and excludes transactions by government entities that are run on a commercial basis. The national accounts measure also consolidates the civil service pension plans with the accounts of the federal and provincial governments.

6. Between 1987 and 1993 the structural deficit remained stubbornly in the range of 4 to 5 per cent of GDP following a drop from its 1985 peak level of $6\frac{1}{2}$ per cent.

7. This is not to say that there may not be moves to reform the tax system, but rather that the motivation behind any changes will be to rationalise or simplify the system rather than raise additional revenue. Indeed, in the recent provincial election in Ontario the Progressive Conservative party was elected on a pledge to reduce the provincial income tax rate by 30 per cent over three years.

8. This would correspond to a deficit of the order of 2 per cent of GDP on a national accounts basis.

9. A number of studies suggest that the macroeconomic effects of fiscal consolidation are more favourable when greater reliance is placed on expenditure cuts rather than increases in taxes; see for example: "Fiscal Restructuring in the Group of Seven Major Industrial Countries in the 1990s: Macroeconomic Effects", L. Bartolini, A. Razin and S. Symansky, IMF Working Paper, March 1995.

10. If real GDP were to remain flat, at the level of the first quarter of 1995, throughout 1995/96, this would imply real growth of about 1 per cent compared to the previous financial year – a reduction of 2.8 per cent per annum relative to the assumption for growth in the Budget. According to the sensitivity analysis tables provided in the Budget Plan, such a reduction in growth would be expected to add about C\$ 3½ billion to the federal deficit. However, the offsetting effect of a fall in interest rates by 2 percentage points would reduce the deficit by a similar amount.

11. The only clear outlier in the relationship between indebtedness, credit ratings and interest rate spreads illustrated in Figure 18 is Quebec, probably reflecting an additional premium associated with the risk of separation from the rest of Canada. Quebec received a further credit downgrading from Moodys (from A1 to A2) in June 1995, which is not reflected in Figure 18.

12. This relationship is summarised by the "government's dynamic budget constraint", see Annex V for details.

13. For the purposes of this calculation the projection of the real economy is assumed to be unchanged.

14. For a comparison of the sensitivity of government finances across different OECD economies to changes in interest rates and growth see OECD *Economic Outlook No. 56*, December 1994.

15. These calculations also assume that potential output growth is also lower by the same amount. If the average GDP growth rate were reduced by ½ per cent per annum, but potential growth rate was assumed to be unaffected, the effect on the government's fiscal position would be less serious and more difficult to assess. The implied increase in the output gap relative to the baseline should result in lower inflation and would therefore allow some easing of monetary conditions and hence potential savings on debt servicing.

16. Namely that of a sustained reduction in government current expenditures by the equivalent of 1 per cent of GDP, using a feedback rule for short-term interest rates which respond to target the inflation rate (thus a fall in the inflation rate is followed by an easing of monetary conditions).

17. Similar results are found in a number of papers, using a range of different models of the Canadian economy, in the conference volume "Debt Reduction: What Pain, What Gain?", eds. W.B.P. Robson and W.M. Scarth, C.D. Howe Institute, Policy Study No. 23, 1994.

18. See "Fiscal Policy, Government Debt and Economic Performance", W. Liebfritz, D. Roseveare and P. van den Noord, OECD Economics Department *Working paper No. 144*, Paris, 1994, and also "Government Deficits, Debt and the Business Cycle",

T. Bayoumi and D. Laxton in "Deficit Reduction. What Pain, What Gain?", eds. W.B.P. Robson and W.M. Scarth, C.D. Howe Institute Policy Study No. 23, 1994.

19. See OECD *Economic Outlook*, June 1995, No. 57, pp. 33-42.

20. On the basis of a survey of the available empirical work, Rose concluded that the 1971 reforms probably added up to 2 percentage points to the NAIRU, see "The NAIRU in Canada: Concepts, Determinants and Estimates", D. Rose, Technical report No. 50, Ottawa, Bank of Canada, 1988.

21. A number of attempts have been made to combine all the various elements of the UI system into a single index of UI generosity. According to one such measure, as a result of a series of marginal reductions in generosity over the last two decades, the overall generosity of UI is now only a little higher than it was before the 1971 reforms, but the dispersion in generosity across the provinces has widened. See "An Index of the Generosity of Unemployment Insurance", T. Sargent, mimeo, Department of Finance, 1995.

22. See "The Causes of Unemployment in Canada: A Review of the Evidence", by S. Poloz, Bank of Canada, Working Paper 94-11, 1994.

23. The effect of taxes on the NAIRU arises when their incidence is borne by employers as an increase in real wage costs, rather than by employees as a reduction in take-home wages. Thus, if an increase in payroll taxes was closely tied to a corresponding increase in prospective benefits, so that employees readily accepted a decline in their take-home pay, then there should be no effect on the NAIRU.

24. See chapter 9 of the "The OECD Jobs Study: Evidence and Explanations. The Adjustment potential of the Labour Market", OECD, Paris, 1994.

25. For example, according to the equations incorporated in the OECD Secretariat"s INTER-LINK macroeconometric model every percentage point rise in payroll taxes "temporarily" increases the NAIRU by more than 4 percentage point years. Thus, unemployment would have to rise by 1 percentage point for four years, or $1/2$ percentage point for eight years (or some similar combination) in order to prevent any long-run change in inflation. According to similar calculations for the other major OECD economies, Canada is one of the most vulnerable to a rise in payroll taxes. The basis for these calculation is described in "The Effect of the Wedge and Productivity on The NAIRU in Five Major OECD Economies" by D. Turner and S. Rauffet, ESRC Macroeconomic Modelling Bureau Discussion Paper No. 38, November 1994.

26. There has been a marginal reduction in payroll taxes at the beginning of 1995 (involving a cut in the employees premium rate from 3.07 to 3 per cent of gross earnings). But the government has made further reductions dependent on build-up of a surplus on the UI account of about C$ 5 to 6 billion, which maybe achieved at the end of 1996.

27. Following the 1994 Budget, the minimum qualifying period of work required is between 12 and 20 weeks of employment during the past year (depending on the regional unemployment rate), the maximum duration of benefits is between 14 and 50 weeks (depending on weeks of prior employment and the regional unemployment rate) and the benefit rate (paid to all except low-income beneficiaries) is 55 per cent of previous earnings.

28. Conversely, the reforms to the UI system in the 1990 Budget, while lowering the overall generosity of the system, concentrated on reducing generosity in the low unemployment regions, thus accentuating regional differentiation.

29. "Improving Social Security in Canada: A Discussion Paper", Government of Canada, Ottawa, 1994.

30. Also, some caution needs to be exercised in interpreting cross-country data on expenditure on passive and active labour market measures because of the problem of standardisation. In the case of Canada, for example, the figures only include expenditures by the federal government and not by provincial governments.

31. See Plamondon & Associates, Inc., "GST Compliance Costs for Small Business in Canada: A Study for the Department of Finance", Tax Policy (1994).

32. A direct personal expenditure tax is applied to the difference between income and savings for each individual on a periodic basis. A further reason why the Committee was reluctant to recommend such a tax is that it has not been adopted anywhere else in the world. A business transfer tax is a subtraction-method VAT which uses the difference between business revenue and purchases of inputs as the tax base.

33. "The Uruguay Round of the General Agreement on Tariffs and Trade: An Assessment of the Economic Impact on Canada", Department of Finance, August 1994.

34. These developments are discussed in Harris (1993).

35. The composition of Canadian output includes somewhat less manufacturing and more mining, construction and services than most industrial economies. For a full discussion of these differences, see McFetridge (1986).

36. A more detailed discussion of these industrial organisation characteristics is provided by West (1994).

37. See Statistics Canada (1993).

38. Crown corporations might be thought of as government-owned enterprises which have been designated as agents of the Crown for the attainment of public policy objectives with the state itself being responsible for all liabilities, according to the definition provided in Borins and Boothman (1986).

39. See Statistics Canada (1993).

40. Statistics Canada, *The Daily*, "Productivity, Hourly Compensation and Unit Labour Cost", 21 April 1995.

41. See Denny, *et al.* (1992).

42. See Charette, Henry and Kaufmann (1985). Any such comparison, if it is to be meaningful, presumes that the countries being compared are subject to the same incentives for structural realignment; *e.g.* similar changes in technology, trade regimes and so forth. It also assumes that the initial underlying structures are relatively similar. While the former assumption seems realistic, the latter is not, and results of the comparison must be interpreted with this qualification in mind.

43. OECD (1992).

44. Gera and Mang (1995).

45. This is suggested by output growth decomposition analysis.

46. Baldwin and Rafiquzzaman (1994), Prasad (1993) and Gera, Caldwell and Ferguson (1993).

47. See "Industrial Policy in OECD Countries. Annual Review 1994", OECD, 1994, p. 138, Table 28.

48. For a discussion of these Reports, see Barrows (1992). The Reports also rank Canada poorly on commitment to human resource skills development and international orientation.

49. See McMillan (1992).

50. Analysis of patent data is provided in Ellis and Waite (1985).

51. For one extensive review, see McFetridge and Corvari (1985).

52. This measure does not net out, however, the effect of foreign affiliates discussed in the preceding paragraph.

53. While direct R&D expenditure is the conventional measure for an industry's technology intensity, some firms and industries may be able to obtain productivity benefits by purchasing and using technologically-sophisticated inputs and capital goods. In Canada, acquired R&D is most important in high-technology sectors such as communication equipment, the semi-conductor and the computer industry, as well as shipbuilding and aerospace (see OECD, 1994). However, as these sectors occupy a small overall share in Canadian output, the effects of indirect R&D on total manufacturing productivity performance are likely to be limited.

54. Many of the relevant studies are reviewed in Bernstein (1985). More recent evidence is provided in OECD (1995).

55. Furthermore, estimated productivity effects of R&D for the United States are comparable to those for Canada, notwithstanding the much higher (absolutely and relatively) rate of R&D spending in the United States. This latter observation suggests that the net benefits of increasing R&D activities in Canada in terms of improvements in productivity may be substantial.

56. One study (Hanel, 1994) even finds a negative correlation between federal R&D subsidies and TFP growth in Canada. It concluded that there is no evidence that industries that benefited from federal grants were more productive than those that did not.

57. The existence of positive externalities to R&D performance is well established. For Canadian evidence, see Bernstein (1988).

58. For a review of some studies, see Bernstein (1985).

59. See Statistics Canada (1995, p. 4).

60. These various criticisms are discussed in Porter (1991).

61. See Daly and Globerman (1976).

62. See Globerman, Ries and Vertinsky (1994).

63. Deregulation has also contributed to firms acknowledging consumer requirements and tastes much more enthusiastically than before. The Canadian experiences with respect to deregulation of the telecommunications and transportation industries are discussed in Globerman (1991) and Palmer (1991) respectively.

64. The relevant evidence is reviewed in West (1994).

65. See, for example, Halpern and Mintz (1991).

66. Overall assessments of the federal and provincial government regional development programmes have difficulty drawing conclusions whether they have helped to promote industrial restructuring. See Savoie (1992).

67. Government of Canada (1994). See also Government of Canada (1995).

68. For a full discussion of the evidence supporting these assertions, see Acs and Audretsch (1990).

69. "Small" Canadian enterprises are understood to include businesses with fewer than 100 employees in manufacturing and fewer than 50 employees in other sectors, while "medium-sized" businesses are those with 100 to 500 employees. In Canada, the SMEs account for 99 per cent of registered businesses, two-thirds of private-sector employment and 60 per cent of GDP.

70. See Lynch (1994, p. 48).

71. For example, a survey of almost 750 US companies by Arthur Andersen & Co. and National Small Business United found that 20 per cent of firms with fewer than 500 employees exported products and services in 1994. While this estimate is not directly comparable to the Canadian data cited in this section, it is suggestive of a stronger involvement in international markets on the part of US SMEs. See "It's a Small (Business) World", *Business Week*, 17 April, 1995, p. 97.

72. Industry Canada estimates that approximately 30 000 firms (3 per cent) are "active innovators" and some 60 000 are "active exporters". It should be noted, however, that active innovation does not necessarily imply the performance of formal R&D.

73. See Lynch (1994, p. 49).

74. Baldwin and Sabourin (1995).

75. Baldwin and Sabourin (1995).

76. An important concern of Canadian authorities has always been that Canadian corporate tax rates remain competitive with those of trading partners, especially the United States. By the early 1990s, however, the effective tax burden on capital in Canada had exceeded that in its neighbouring country, taking into account tax rates, depreciation allowances and inventory deductions. One estimate puts the average (effective) rate across a set of two-digit industries for 1990 at approximately 30 per cent for Canada and 20 per cent for the United States (see Halpern and Mintz, 1991).

77. See Small Business Working Committee (1994).

78. A recent survey by the Canadian Federation of Independent Business (CFIB) estimated that loan refusal rates had increased from 9 per cent in 1988 to 14 per cent in 1994.

79. Thus, if a firm is non-taxable, a tax credit has no immediate value unless the R&D credit is refundable to the firm or the unused credit can flow through to taxable investors. In fact, full refunds are extended to Canadian-controlled private corporations with taxable income under $200 000 on the credits earned in respect of the first $2 million of qualifying R&D expense in a year. See Brean (1994).

80. Evidence on the potential importance of these latter factors is provided in Good and Graves (1993).

81. See Baldwin and Johnson (1994).

82. See Picot (1994).

83. A recent survey (Statistics Canada, 1994) which focused on differences among more-successful and less-successful Canadian SMEs identified the innovation capabilities of a firm and an aggressive focus on new (especially export) markets as key features distinguishing the two sets of firms.

84. Government of Canada (1994).

85. Within the small business procurement plan proposed by the government *i)* small and aboriginal companies will gain exclusive access to all contracts below C$ 125 000 when qualified and cost-effective suppliers can be found; *ii)* they will also be preferred bidders on contracts over C$ 125 000, including subcontracts, where the potential exists to support or develop innovative firms; *iii)* aboriginal companies will get a first crack at work destined for native populations; *iv)* a pilot project will use government procurement to develop new products and technologies.

86. For a full review of the policy context, as well as an economic evaluation of the link between economic performance and the information highway, see Globerman (1995).

87. On this point, see Evans and Karras (1994), Holtz-Eakin (1994) and Nadiri and Mumaneas (1994).

88. With respect to the information highway, in particular, it has been argued that the development of new infrastructures and multimedia applications can be expected to generate a number of new activities and transform, or substitute for, existing ones, so that it is difficult to make productivity predictions using historical data.

89. See, for example Ford and Poret (1991). The authors do not find, however, any effect in the United States and most other countries and conclude that, overall, their results are not robust enough to support a policy recommendation of an acceleration of infrastructure investment.

90. See Postner (1993).

91. This argument is made in Globerman (1995).

92. Specifically, the government through the issuance of an Order-In-Council asked the Canadian Radio-television and Telecommunications Commission (CRTC) to recommend rules for competition between cable and telephone companies in the provision of local distribution network services. The regulatory basis for such competition was established in a 1994 decision by the CRTC opening up the local telephone sector to competition. Remaining regulation focuses on the price of monopoly services and potential abuse of market dominance.

93. The modifications of the NAFTA with respect to Canada-US trade relations are relatively modest as they relate more to procedural matters than to the scope and magnitude of trade liberalisation. For an assessment of Canada's interests in the NAFTA and how NAFTA modifies the FTA, see Globerman (1993).

94. See Schwanen (1992).

95. For a review and evaluation of the evidence linking outward foreign direct investment to industrial restructuring in the home country, see Globerman (1994).

96. Promoting internal trade through the elimination of inter-provincial barriers is also a government priority, as discussed in Chapter III.

97. For an overview of how the existing NAFTA might be "widened and deepened", see Hufbauer (1994).

98. Although the APEC organisation as a group has neither the mechanisms in place, nor the commitment to promote free trade among its members, it serves as a potential forum for stimulating trade among them.

99. For a wide-ranging critique of Canadian federal and provincial government science and technology programmes, see Palda (1993). Particular concerns of small business are discussed in Baetz and Craig (1989).

Bibliography

Acs, Zoltan J. and David B. Audretsch, *Innovation and Small Firms,* Cambridge, Mass.: The MIT Press, 1990.

Baetz, Mark and Ron Craig, "The Role of Government in Manufacturing Automation: The Views and Experience of Small Versus Large Business," *Journal of Small Business Entrepreneurship,* Vol. 7, October/December 1989, pp. 17-27.

Baldwin, John and Canadian Institute for Advanced Research, "Innovation: The Key to Success in Small Firms", mimeo, undated.

Baldwin, John and Joanne Johnson, "Human Capital Development and Innovation: The Case of Training in Small and Medium-Sized Enterprises", Statistics Canada, 1984, mimeo.

Baldwin, John and M. Rafiquzzaman, "Structural Change in the Canadian Manufacturing Sector", Paper presented at Canadian Association of Business Economists' Session on Economic Restructuring in the Canadian Economy, 5 June 1994.

Baldwin, John, and D. Sabourin, *Technology Adoption in Canadian Manufacturing,* Statistics Canada, Ottawa, 1995.

Barrows, David, "Canada's Global Competitiveness," in Jerry Dermer, ed., *Meeting the Global Challenge: Competitive Position and Strategic Response,* Toronto: Captus Press Inc., 1992, pp. 32-63.

Bernstein, Jeffrey I., "Research and Development, Patent and Grant and Tax Policies in Canada", in D.G. McFetridge, ed., *Technological Change in Canadian Industry,* Toronto: University of Toronto Press, 1985, pp. 1-42.

Bernstein, Jeffrey I., "Costs of Production, Intraindustry and Interindustry R&D Spillovers: Canadian Evidence", *Canadian Journal of Economics,* Vol. 21, No. 2, 1988, pp. 324-347.

Borins, Sanford and Barry Boothman, "Crown Corporations and Economic Efficiency", in Donald McFetridge, ed., *Canadian Industrial Policy in Action*, Toronto: University of Toronto Press, 1986.

Charette, Michael F., Robert P. Henry and Barry Kaufmann, "The Evolution of the Canadian Industrial Structure: An International Perspective", in D.G. McFetridge, ed., *Canadian Industry in Transition,* Toronto: University of Toronto Press, 1985, pp. 61-134.

Chow, Franklin, "Recent Trends in Canadian Direct Investment Abroad", in Steven Globerman, ed., *Canadian-Based Multinationals,* Calgary: University of Calgary Press, 1994, pp. 35-62.

Daly, D.J., and S. Globerman, *Tariffs and Science Policies: Application of a Model of Economic Nationalism,* Toronto: University of Toronto Press, 1976.

Denny, M., J. Bernstein, M. Fuss, S Nakamura, and L. Waverman, "Productivity in Manufacturing Industries, Canada, Japan and the United States, 1953-1986: Was the Productivity Slowdown Reversed?", *Canadian Journal of Economics,* Vol. XXV, N 3, August 1992, pp. 584-603.

Department of Regional Industrial Expansion, "Canada's Industrial Adjustment: Federal Government Policies and Programs", in John Whalley with Roderick Hill, eds., *Domestic Policies in the International Economic Environment,* Toronto: University of Toronto Press, 1985, pp. 215-42.

Ellis, Ned and David Waite, "Canadian Technological Output in a World Context", in D.G. McFetridge, ed., *Technological Change in Canadian Industry,* Toronto: University of Toronto Press, 1975, pp. 43-75.

Evans, Paul, and Georgios Karras, "Are Government Activities Productive? Evidence from a Panel of U.S. States", The Review of Economics and Statistics, Vol. LXXVI, No. 1, 1994, pp. 1-11.

Ford, R., and P. Poret, "Infrastructure and Private-Sector Productivity", OECD *Working Paper No. 91,* January 1991.

Fortin, Pierre, "Slow Growth, Unemployment and Debt: What Happened? What Can We Do?", in Thomas Courchene, ed., *Stabilization, Growth and Distribution: Linkages in the Knowledge Era,* Kingston: John Deutsch Institute for the Study of Economic Policy, 1994, pp. 67-108.

Gera, Surendra, David Caldwell and David Ferguson, "Industrial Restructuring in Canadian Manufacturing: A Comparison of the Early 1980s and 1990s", Paper presented at the Canadian Economics Association meeting, 4 to 6 June 1993.

Gera, Surendra, and Kurt Mang, "Changing Canadian Industrial Structure", May 1995.

Globerman Steven, "Deregulation of Telecommunications: An Assessment", in Walter Block and George Lermer, eds., *Breaking the Shackles: Deregulating Canadian Industry,* Vancouver: The Fraser Institute, 1991, pp. 87-131.

Globerman, Steven, "Formal Education and the Adaptability of Workers and Managers to Technological Change", in Craig Riddell, ed., *Studies in Labor Markets, Ottawa: Supply and Services Canada,* 1985, pp. 41-69.

Globerman, Steven, "The Information Highway and the Economy", Paper presented at Industry Canada Conference on Knowledge-Based Economic Growth, Ottawa, 31 March 1995.

Globerman, Steven, "The Private and Social Interests in Outward Direct Investment", in Steven Globerman, ed., *Canadian-Based Multinationals,* Calgary: University of Calgary Press, 1994, pp. 1-34.

Globerman, Steven, "Canada's Interest in North American Economic Integration", *Canadian Public Administration,* Vol. 36, No. 1, 1993, pp. 90-105.

Globerman, Steven, John Ries, and Ilan Vertinsky, "The Economic Performance of Foreign-Owned Affiliates in Canada", *Canadian Journal of Economics,* Vol. XXVII, No. 7, 1994, pp. 143-156.

Good, Walter and J. Robert Graves, "Small-Business Support Programs: The Views of Failed Versus Surviving Firms", *Journal of Small Business and Entrepreneurship,* Vol. 10, January/ March 1993, pp. 66-76.

Government of Canada, "Agenda: Jobs and Growth, Building a More Innovative Economy", Ottawa: Minister of Supply and Services Canada, 1994.

Government of Canada, "Healthy, Wealthy and Wise: A Framework for an Integrated Federal Science and Technology Strategy", Report of the National Advisory Board on Science and Technology, Ottawa, 1995.

Halpern, Paul and Jack Mintz, "Taxation and Canada-U.S. Cross-Border Acquisitions", in Leonard Waverman, ed., *Corporate Globalisation Through Mergers and Acquisitions,* Calgary: University of Calgary Press, 1991, pp. 153-94.

Hanel, Petr, "R&D, Interindustry and International Spill-overs of Technology and TFP Growth of Canadian Manufacturing Industries", Research Paper 94-04, University of Sherbrooke, Canada, October 1994.

Harris, Richard, "Presidential Address: Globalization, Trade and Income", *Canadian Journal of Economics*, Vol. XXVI, No. 4, November 1993, pp. 755-776.

Harris, Richard, *Trade, Industrial Policy and International Competition,* Toronto: University of Toronto Press, 1985.

Holtz-Eakin, Douglas, "Public Sector Capital and the Productivity Puzzle", *The Review of Economics and Statistics*, Vol. LXXVI, No. 1, 1994, pp. 12-21.

Hufbauer, Gary C., "Deeper and Wider: An Agenda for NAFTA", *Northwest Journal of Business and Economics, Special Edition,* 1994, pp. 31-40.

Lynch, Kevin, "Challenges of the New Global Economy", *CGA Magazine,* May 1994.

McFetridge, Donald, "The Economics of Industrial Structure: An Overview", in D.G. McFetridge, ed., *Canadian Industry in Transportation,* Toronto: University of Toronto Press, 1986.

McFetridge, Donald and R. J. Corvari, "Technology Diffusion: A Survey of Canadian Evidence and Public Policy Issues", in D.G. McFetridge, ed., *Technological Change in Canadian Industry,* Toronto: University of Toronto Press, 1975, pp. 177-231.

McMillan, Charles J., "Technology and Competitiveness: A Canadian Strategy", in Jerry Dermer, ed., *Meeting the Global Challenge: Competitive Position and Strategic Response,* Toronto: Captus Press Inc., 1992, pp. 87-116.

Nadiri, M. Ishaq and Theofanis P. Mumaneas, "The Effects of Public Infrastructure and R&D Capital on the Cost Structure and Performance of US Manufacturing Industries", *The Review of Economics and Statistics,* Vol. LXXVI, No. 1, 1994, pp. 22-35.

Organisation for Economic Development and Co-operation, *Structural change and Industrial Performance,* Paris: OECD, 1992.

Organisation for Economic Development and Co-operation, *Technology Diffusion and Industrial Performance,* unpublished, 1994.

Organisation for Economic Development and Co-operation, *The Impact of R&D and Technology Diffusion on Productivity Growth: Evidence for 10 OECD countries in the 1970s and 1980s,* OECD: Paris, 1995.

Palda, Kristian, *Innovation Policy and Canada's Competitiveness,* Vancouver: The Fraser Institute, 1993.

Palmer, John, ''Truck and Rail Shipping: The Deregulation Evolution'', in Walter Block and George Lermer, eds., *Breaking the Shackles: Deregulating Canadian Industry,* Vancouver: The Fraser Institute, 1991, pp. 151-69.

Picot, G., J. Baldwin, and R. Dupuy, *Have Small Firms Created a Disproportionate share of New Jobs in Canada?* CEA Meeting paper, Calgary, 1994.

Porter, Michael E., *Canada at the Crossroads: The Reality of a New Competitive Environment,* Ottawa: Business Council on National Issues, 1991.

Postner, Harry H., ''A Note on Infrastructure and Productivity'', Kingston: Queen's University Discussion Paper No. 93-12, 1993.

Prasad, Eswar, ''Labor Market Aspects of Industrial Restructuring in Canada'', Paper presented at Canadian Economics Association meetings, 5 June 1993.

Savoie, Donald J., *Regional Economic Development: Canada's Search for Solutions,* 2nd Edition, Toronto: University of Toronto Press, 1992.

Schwanen, Daniel; *Were the Optimists Wrong About Free Trade?,* Toronto: C.D. Howe Research Institute, 1994.

Small Business Working Committee, *Breaking Through Barriers:* Forging Our Future, Ottawa: Industry Canada, 1994.

Statistics Canada, *Federal Scientific Activities 1994-95,* Ottawa: Supply and Services Canada, 1995.

Statistics Canada, *Industrial Research and Development,* Ottawa: Supply and Services Canada, 1995.

Statistics Canada, *Strategies for Success. A Profile of Growing Small and Medium-fixed Enterprises in Canada,* Ottawa, 1994.

Statistics Canada, *Parliamentary Report of the Ministry of Industry, Science and Technology Under the Corporations and Labour Unions Return Act,* Part I – Corporations: Foreign Control in the Canadian Economy, Ottawa; December 1993.

West, Douglas S., *Modern Canadian Industrial Organization,* Second Edition, Harper Collins College Publishers, 1994.

Annex I

Explaining changes in inflation

This annex describes the estimation of an equation, reported in Table A1 below, which explains changes in CPI inflation (excluding food and energy) as referred to in Chapter I of the main text. The equation specification has been chosen to largely coincide with that reported in "Empirical evidence on the strength of the monetary transmission mechanism in Canada", by Pierre Duguay, *Journal of Monetary Economics*, Volume 33, No. 1. The equation reported here is based on a more up-to-date sample which ends in 1994, rather than 1990 in the case of Duguay.

Table A2 compares the long-run elasticities from the equation reported in Table A1 with those from Duguay (1994). The effect of the output gap variable is smaller in the Secretariat equation, implying a sacrifice ratio of 2.3 rather than 1.7. There is also a difference between the effect of the exchange rate in the two equations. According to the Secretariat equation the effect of a once-for-all change in the real exchange rate has a permanent effect on the inflation rate: a permanent once-for-all change in the real exchange rate of 10 per cent permanently increases the steady state inflation rate by about 2 per cent per annum (independently of any effect operating through changes in demand). Conversely, according to the Duguay equation there is only a temporary effect on inflation from a change in the real exchange rate consistent with a rise in the consumer price level of about 2 per cent (which is roughly equivalent to the import share of the Canadian CPI basket).

The finding of a permanent effect from the real exchange rate on inflation suggests that there is a further transmission mechanism at work in addition to the simple direct effect of increased import prices being passed on directly in higher consumer prices (which would imply only a "temporary" effect on inflation). One possibility is "real wage resistance", which arises when employees attempt to maintain the value of their real consumption wage following an increase in any component of the "wedge" (including import prices as well as taxes) between employer's real wage costs and real consumption wages. Evidence of real wage resistance in Canada is present in the wage equations reported in "Unemployment: Macroeconomic Performance and the Labour Market", by R. Layard, S. Nickell and R. Jackman, Oxford University Press, 1991. Real wage resistance is also a feature of the estimated wage equation included in the OECD Secretariat's INTERLINK model.

The main effects acting on inflation since 1990 can be quantified using the estimated equation reported in Table A1. There are, however, a number of caveats to using an estimated equation to interpret the recent changes in inflation. First, price increases over much of the recent period have been at historically low levels and it is possible that they are less responsive (particularly in a downwards direction) at very low levels of inflation. Moreover, to the extent that increased crèdibility is attached to the Bank of Canada's inflation targets, past empirical relationships may be a poor guide to explaining recent changes in inflation. The equation estimates are also sensitive to estimates of the output gap over which considerable uncertainty is inevitably attached, particularly over the recent period in which considerable restructuring has taken place, see Parker "Aspects of economic restructuring in Canada", *Bank of Canada Review*, Summer 1995.

Definition of variables used in Table A1

Inflation	=	Change in the quarterly inflation rate of the CPI (excluding food and energy).
Output gap	=	OECD Secretariat estimates of the Output gap.
Real oil price	=	(Logged) Oil price relative to CPI.
Indirect taxes	=	Effective indirect tax rate.
Dummy 91Q1	=	Dummy variable associated with major change indirect taxes in 1991, taking the value +1 in 1991 Q1 and –1 in 1991 Q2 and zero elsewhere.
Real exchange rate	=	Real Canadian-US exchange rate, based on relative CPI's (defined as the Canadian dollar price of the US dollar multiplied by the US CPI and divided by the Canadian CPI).

Details of diagnostic tests reported in Table A1

Serial Correlation:	A Lagrange multiplier test for up to fourth order Serial correlation.
Functional Form:	Ramsey's RESET test using the square of fitted values.
Normality:	Jarque-Bera test for normality of the residuals, testing skewness and kurtosis of residuals.
Heteroscedasticity:	Based on the regression of squared residuals on squared fitted values.
Predictive Failure:	Chow's second test, estimating the equation over the full sample and a sample in which the observations from 1990 Q1 onwards are omitted.
Chow test:	A chow test for structural stability, dividing the estimation period in half.

Table A1. **Estimation results of inflation equation**

Dependent variable: Change in the rate of quarterly CPI (excluding food and energy) inflation
Sample period: 1972 Q2-1994 Q3 (t-statistics in brackets)

Constant	0.002	(2.4)
Lagged output gap$_{-1}$	0.061	(4.6)
Δ Output gap$_{-1}$	0.038	(1.0)
Lagged Δ inflation		
−1	−0.599	(−6.9)
−2	−0.466	(−4.3)
−3	−0.139	(−1.5)
Δ Real exchange rate (logged)		
−1	0.087	(4.1)
−3	0.032	(1.6)
Δ Real oil prices (logged)		
−1	0.006	(1.7)
−3	0.011	(2.9)
−4	−0.007	(−1.9)
Δ Indirect taxes		
0	0.290	(3.7)
−1	0.163	(2.0)
−5	−0.133	(−1.8)
Dummy 91 Q1	0.018	(5.8)
Seasonal dummies		
Q1	−0.006	(−5.4)
Q2	−0.001	(−1.2)
Q3	−0.002	(−2.0)
R^2	0.70	
Standard error of equation ($\times$ 100)	0.30	
Serial correlation	$F_{(4,68)} = 0.32$	
Functional form	$F_{(1,71)} = 0.19$	
Normality	$\chi^2(2) = 3.10$	
Heteroscedasticity	$F_{(1,88)} = 0.71$	
Predictive failure (from 1990 Q1)	$F_{(19,54)} = 0.63$	
Chow test (break at 1983 Q2)	$F_{(17.56)} = 0.62$	

Table A2. Long-run elasticities of reduced form inflation equations

	Equation in Table A1	Duguay (1994)
Output gap	0.11	0.15
(Sacrifice ratio)	(2.26)	(1.68)
Real exchange rate	0.21	0.0[1]
Real oil price	0.004	0.008
Indirect taxes	0.58	0.36

1. In Duguay's equation there is no permanent effect on the inflation rate from a change in the real exchange rate, although there is a permanent effect on the price level with a long-run elasticity of about 0.2 (see text for discussion).
Source: The elasticities in the second column are taken from the final equation in Table 2 of Duguay (1994).

Nevertheless, the estimated equation does seem to be capable of explaining much of the change in inflation since 1990 (see Table A3*i*, A3*ii* and Figure 8 in Chapter I). Thus, consumer price inflation rose by about 1$^{1}/_{2}$ per cent per annum between 1990 and 1991, mainly as a consequence of the rise in indirect taxes associated with the introduction of the Goods and Services Tax (GST) and despite output falling from a level of about 3 per cent above potential in 1990 to nearly 3$^{1}/_{2}$ per cent below in 1991. In 1992, the rate of consumer price inflation fell by nearly 4 percentage points to about 2 per cent per annum, as the output gap continued to widen to about 5 percentage points and the impact effect of indirect tax changes dropped out the calculation of inflation. Lagged effects from a fall in real oil prices may also have contributed about $^{1}/_{2}$ per cent to the fall in inflation in 1992.

Table A3*i*. Factors underlying changes in consumer price inflation
1990-1994

	Consumer price inflation [1] (Per cent per annum)	Output gap [2] (Per cent points)	Real exchange rate [3] (1990 = 100)	Indirect tax rate [4] (Per cent)	Real oil price [5] (1990 = 100)
1990	4.4	+3.2	100.0	19.4	100.0
1991	5.8	−3.4	101.6	22.0	81.2
1992	2.1	−5.0	104.3	22.6	78.1
1993	2.0	−5.1	112.8	22.8	77.7
1994	0.1	−3.2	122.7	20.9	77.5

1. Inflation is measured according to the consumer price index, excluding food and energy, but not excluding indirect taxes.
2. The output gap figures are OECD Secretariat estimates: a negative figure implies that GDP is below potential output.
3. The real exchange rate is measured as the real Canadian-US exchange rate based on relative CPIs: a higher value implies an improvement in the competitiveness of Canadian goods and increased inflationary pressure from import prices.
4. The indirect tax rate is that for the CPI excluding energy and food.
5. The real oil price is the imported price of oil (in domestic currency) relative to the CPI.
Source: Bank of Canada, Statistics Canada and OECD Secretariat estimates.

Table A3*ii*. **Explaining the changes in consumer price inflation**

1990-94

| | (1)
Change
in inflation | Explained by changes in: [1] | | | | (6)
Total
explained | (7)
Unex-
plained
residual |
		(2) Output gap	(3) Real exchange rate	(4) Indirect taxes	(5) Real oil price		
1991/90	1.4	−0.5	−0.3	2.9	0.2	2.2	−0.8
1992/91	−3.8	−1.9	0.1	−0.9	−0.5	−3.1	−0.7
1993/92	−0.1	−2.4	2.0	−0.2	0.2	−0.3	0.2
1994/93	−1.9	−2.1	1.8	−1.2	−0.2	−1.6	−0.3

1. Calculations based on the equation reported in Table A1. Definition and source of variables correspond to those given in Table A3*i*. Column (6) is the sum of columns (2) to (5). Column (7) equals column (6) minus column (1).

In both 1993 and 1994 the disinflationary effect of the large output gap, which *ceteris paribus* might have been expected to reduce the annual inflation rate by between 2 and 2½ per cent in each year, was largely offset by the inflationary effect of the depreciation of the real exchange rate. Although inflation did fall in 1994, this can largely be attributed to the effect of a reduction in indirect taxes.

Annex II

Speed limit and asymmetric inflation effects

The present annex first examines some evidence regarding the existence of a "speed limit" effect from closing the output gap, which is referred to briefly in Chapter II. It then provides further details of the simulations reported in this chapter, which contrast results from a variant of the OECD Secretariat's INTERLINK model for Canada, allowing for "asymmetric" effects from the output gap on inflation, with the standard model.

Speed limit effects from the output gap on inflation

The disinflationary effect of any output gap may be reduced if the output gap is in the process of closing, [see Turner (1995)]. In an extreme case it is conceivable that if the output is being closed very rapidly then there may be some positive pressure on inflation, even though output remains below potential output.

In order to examine the possible scale of such a "speed limit" effect the disinflationary effect of the output gap is calculated according to the reduced form inflation equation reported in Table A1. The short-term projections discussed in Chapter I imply that the slowdown in growth in 1995 leads to some widening of the output gap, but that from the beginning of 1996 the gap begins to close again. Four scenarios are considered in which it is assumed that the output gap in 1995 Q4 is 2½ per cent and that it is closed at a steady rate in either 1, 4, 8 or 12 quarters. Thus, for each of the four scenarios, Table A4 reports the disinflationary effect and the implied sacrifice ratio. In every case the implied sacrifice ratio is higher than the steady state value of 2.26: the faster the output gap is closed, the smaller the disinflationary effect relative to the loss in output. A speed limit effect is calculated in the final column of Table A4 as the proportion by which the disinflationary effect of the gap is diminished as a result of closing the gap quickly.

However, even in the most extreme case where the output gap is closed in a single quarter, the speed limit effect is only 62 per cent, well short of the 100 per cent which would be required if there was to be positive inflationary pressure from the output gap. In the more realistic case where the output gap is closed in 4 quarters (which on OECD Secretariat estimates would still require growth of over 5 per cent per annum throughout 1996), the speed limit effect is only 25 per cent. If the same calculations are repeated, but using the equation estimated by Duguay (referenced in Annex I), then the results are

Table A4. **The speed limit effect from closing the output gap**[1]

(1) Numbers of quarters over which output gap is closed	(2) Cumulative output gap from 1995 Q4 (inclusive) (Per cent point years)	(3) Fall in inflation (Per cent per annum)	(4) Sacrifice ratio (steady-state value is 2.26) = (2)/(3)	(5) Speed limit effect (Per cent)
1	−0.63	−0.10	5.99	62
4	−1.56	−0.52	3.01	25
8	−2.81	−1.07	2.62	14
12	−4.06	−1.62	2.50	10

1. The cumulative output gap is calculated on the assumption that the output gap is −2.5 per cent in 1995 Q4 and that is closed steadily. For example, if the output gap is closed in 4 quarters the output gap is −2.5, −1.88, −1.25, −0.63 and 0.0 in each quarter from 1995 Q4 to 1996 Q4 respectively. The resulting fall in inflation is calculated from the estimated equation reported in Table A1. The speed limit effect is then calculated as the proportionate reduction in the disinflationary effect of the gap in comparison to the reduction in inflation which would have take place assuming that the steady state sacrifice ratio of 2.26 was realised [*i.e.* column (1) divided by 2.26].

similar with speed limit effects of 71, 28, 16 and 11 per cent when the output gap is closed in 1 ,4, 8, and 12 quarters respectively. The absence of strong speed limit effects is also supported by Laxton *et al.* (1992). They find that speed limits most often show up when potential output is essentially drawn as a straight line, but that when estimates of potential allow for a supply component then speed limit effects are difficult to find and economically small.

Asymmetric effects from the output gap on inflation

The presence of asymmetric effects from the output gap on inflation is here taken to mean that the magnitude of the inflationary effect of output being above potential is greater than the disinflationary effect of output being below potential.*

The baseline for both simulations, assumes a "soft-landing" so that the output gap is not closed until 1997, with inflation remaining roughly stable at just under 2 per cent per annum – the disinflationary effect of the output gap roughly offsetting the effect of higher real import prices. Two alternative hard landing variants are also considered. In both cases it is assumed that output initially over-shoots potential as a consequence of rapid growth in 1996-97 (assumed to be the result of higher export demand), but that

---

* The work by Laxton *et al.* (1993, 1994) and Turner (1995) supports the idea that the inflationary effect of output being above potential is greater than the disinflationary effect of output being below potential. In reviewing the evidence for Canada, Poloz (1994) argues that if such findings hold up to further scrutiny, "much of what we now think we know about potential output and the NAIRU may need to be rewritten".

thereafter there is a tightening of monetary and fiscal policy which reduces output below potential, by an amount approximately equivalent to the initial over-shoot. The difference between the two hard-landing scenarios is that, in the first, the standard INTERLINK model is used, whereas in the second a variant is used which allows for an estimated asymmetry in the inflationary effect of positive and negative output gaps. Using the standard INTERLINK model, inflation temporarily peaks just outside the target range, but returns to the mid-point of the range by the end of the scenario (see Figure 14 in Chapter II). However, with asymmetric inflation effects, the consequences of the same shock are very different: inflation increases more markedly as output over-shoots potential and remains well above the target range once policy is tightened, because the disinflationary effects of output being below potential are small in comparison with the inflationary effects of the "over-shoot". These simulations demonstrate that, in the presence of asymmetric inflationary effects from the output gap, the inflationary consequences of allowing output to overshoot potential may be very costly.

Bibliography

Laxton D, K. Shoom and R. Tetlow (1992), "Should the change in the gap appear in the Phillip's curve? Some consequences of mismeasuring potential output", Bank of Canada *Working Paper, 92-2.*

Laxton D., N. Ricketts and D. Rose (1993), "Uncertainty, Learning and Policy Credibility", in "Economic Behaviour and Policy Choice under Price Stability", proceedings of a conference held at the Bank of Canada, October 1993, Bank of Canada.

Laxton D., D. Rose and R. Tetlow (1993a), "Is the Canadian Phillips Curve Non-linear?", Bank of Canada, *Working Paper 93-7.*

Laxton D., G. Meredith and D. Rose (1994), "Asymmetric effects of Economic Activity on Inflation: Evidence and Policy Implications", IMF Working Paper, WP/94/139.

Turner D. (1995), "Speed Limit and Asymmetric Inflation Effects from the Output Gap in the Major Seven Economies", *OECD Economic Studies, 95/1.*

Annex III

The determinants of real long-term interest rates

This annex provides a descriptive summary of recent research by the OECD Secretariat* which attempts to explain developments in real long-term interest rates. An empirical relationship based on this research is used to analyse recent developments in Canadian interest rates in Chapter II.

The research referred to above explains real long-term interest rates in terms of developments in long-run and short-run economic factors in a multi-country framework using a data set covering seventeen OECD countries since the early 1980s. A simultaneous estimation procedure (using instrumental variables) is adopted, with an error-correction framework for each country separating the long-run fundamental influence on real rates from the higher frequency short-term dynamics. Parameters on the long-run variables are constrained to be equal across countries, which imposes the requirement that they have consistent effects both on behaviour through time and explaining cross-country interest differentials.

The long-run component of the real interest rate is modelled as a function of: the rate of return on capital; the government deficit as a proportion of GDP; a measure of the domestic portfolio risk of holding bonds; a five-year moving average of the current account-to-GDP ratio; and the difference between a ten-year moving average of inflation and expected inflation (the latter calculated with a Hodrick-Prescott filter). It is argued that, in a world of mobile capital, it is sensible to treat developments in these long-run variables consistently across variables.

The rate of return on capital is taken to proxy the opportunity cost of holding bonds. The government deficit is taken as an indicator of exogenous influences on net saving trends. For example, a persistent deficit suggests some ex-ante shortage of domestic saving relative to investment, and therefore requiring higher current real interest rates. The empirical results show that an increase in the government budget deficit by the equivalent of 1 percentage point of GDP increases real long-term interest rates by about 15 basis points in the long run.

* Real Long-term Interest Rates: the evidence from pooled time-series'', by A. Orr, M. Edey and M. Kennedy, OECD Economics Department *Working Paper*, 1995. Forthcoming in OECD *Economic Studies, 95/2.*

Other components of the long-run real interest rate may be associated with exchange risk. Thus a history of persistent current account deficits may lead to expectations of a depreciation of the real exchange rate. As in the case of the government budget, the empirical evidence suggests that an increase in the current account deficit by the equivalent of 1 percentage point of GDP increases real long-term interest rates by about 15 basis points in the long-run. Similarly, if the long-run historical performance on inflation relative to existing market expectations is poor, there may be some expectation of future exchange rate depreciation so that some additional yield on bonds may be required.

In addition to these long-run variables, there are a set of country-specific short-run variables which explain movements in long-term interest rates. In the case of Canada, for example, the first difference of changes in US interest rates, the change in inflation and the change in Canadian short-term interest rates all have an effect.

Annex IV

Federal-provincial transfers

This Annex discusses in more detail the existing system of federal-provincial transfers and the reform announced to the system in the 1995 Budget, which will be implemented in 1996/97 (see the fiscal policy section in Chapter II). The main federal transfers to the provinces in 1994/95 accounted for an estimated 22 per cent of total federal programme expenditure and between 20 and 40 per cent of the revenue of individual provinces. The major transfer programmes currently consist of the following:

– *The Established Programs Financing (EPF)*. This represents the largest programme, accounting for 58 per cent of transfers to the provinces in 1994/95. It provides financial support for health and post-secondary education to all provinces on an equal per capita basis. The size of per capita transfers have been frozen in nominal terms since 1990.

– *The Canada Assistance Plan (CAP)*. This programme provides financial support for provincial social assistance and welfare services on the basis of half the expenditure incurred by the provinces. It accounted for 22 per cent of total transfers to the provinces in 1994/95. Its cost-shared nature led to a rapid escalation in the size of the CAP and the imposition of annual limits of 5 per cent on the growth of CAP grants to the three highest income provinces (Alberta, British Columbia and Ontario).

– *Equalisation payments*. This programme is intended to compensate the provinces for differences in their ability to raise revenues, so as to allow for a roughly equivalent level of public services across them. It accounted for 23 per cent of total transfers to the provinces in 1994/95.

Reform of this system of transfer payments has been prompted by concerns that it has fostered an inefficient delivery of social programmes, an inequitable division between provinces and an unwarranted growth both in welfare expenditures and transfer payments to the provinces.

The shared cost nature of the CAP, which implies that provinces only pay half the marginal cost of expanding social assistance and welfare services, has led to a substantial increase in such expenditures. As noted in Chapter III of last year's OECD Survey, it is striking that real spending on social assistance has continued to expand even during periods of strong economic growth. Moreover, given its cost-shared nature, it is not clear that the distribution of transfers under the CAP has necessarily been according to the needs of different provinces, rather than their ability or willingness to finance (part of the cost of) increased social assistance. The criteria for support under the CAP may also have inhibited provinces from providing alternative forms of social assistance, which may have been more appropriate to particular local circumstances. For example, spending on active labour market measures does not qualify for support.

Given the size of these transfers and the federal government's commitment to fiscal consolidation, some reform to limit future growth in this category of expenditure was essential. The 1995 Budget announced that starting in 1996/97 the Canada Health and Social Transfer (CHST) will replace current transfers provided by EPF and CAP, although the system of equalisation payments will remain. The CHST will be entirely in the form of a block-grant, thus eliminating the shared-cost element in the current system of CAP. The provinces will be free to spend the CHST in whatever way they choose, subject only to minimal requirements of meeting national standards for healthcare and to the condition that they continue to provide social assistance without any minimum residency requirements.

The introduction of the new transfer system in 1996/97 will also see a reduction in the overall level of transfers to the provinces, which will decline by the equivalent of about 1 per cent of GDP over two years, see Table A5. Of some concern is how the provinces will react to this future cutback in revenue. During the early 1990s provincial deficits widened considerably, in large part due the unexpected severity of the recession. However, an additional factor which exacerbated this situation was the constraints imposed by the federal government on the growth of transfers to the provinces. Cuts in transfers, particularly over and above those proposed in the 1995 Budget are likely to require a period of adjustment by the provinces. A factor which could potentially hamper adjustment is that a formula for the distribution of the CHST amongst the provinces after 1996/97 has yet to be agreed. This is likely to be a contentious issue as a series of fairly *ad hoc* constraints on the growth of transfers over recent years have distorted the current distribution among the provinces.

Table A5. **Federal transfers to the provinces**

	1993/94	1994/95	1995/96	1996/97	1997/98
	Per cent of GDP[1]				
Current arrangements					
Canada Assistance Plan	1.1	1.1	1.0	–	–
Established Programs Financing	3.0	2.9	2.8	–	–
Total	4.1	3.9	3.8	–	–
Canada Health and Social Transfer	–	–	–	3.3	2.9
Equalisation	1.1	1.1	1.1	1.1	1.1
TOTAL MAJOR TRANSFERS	5.1	5.0	4.8	4.3	3.9

1. For the purpose of these calculations the figures for nominal GDP in 1995/96 and 1996/97 are the 1995 Budget assumptions, and for 1997/98 nominal GDP is then assumed to grow by 5 per cent.
Source: Department of Finance.

Annex V

Further details of fiscal policy simulations presented in Chapter II

The government's dynamic budget constraint

This section derives simple conditions under which debt will remain a constant proportion of GDP. This framework is used both in Table 11 of Chapter II to illustrate the conditions under which the debt-to-GDP ratio will remain stable in the future and also here to analyse the historical deterioration in the debt situation.

Suppose debt remains a constant proportion of GDP over time, so that:

(A1)   DEBT/GDP = Constant,

where DEBT and GDP are both in nominal terms. Then, differentiating (A1) with respect to time, t, gives:

(A2) $1/\text{GDP} \,.\, d\text{DEBT}/dt - \text{DEBT}/\text{GDP} \,.\, 1/\text{GDP} \,.\, d\text{GDP}/dt = 0$

But the change in debt over a given time period, $d\text{DEBT}/dt$, defines the budget deficit (DEFICIT). Also the expression $(1/\text{GDP} \,.\, d\text{GDP}/dt)$ is the growth rate of nominal GDP which can alternatively be expressed as $(g + \pi)$, where g is the growth rate of real GDP and π is the inflation rate. Thus, substituting into (A2) and re-arranging gives:

(A3) $(g + \pi)$ DEBT/GDP = DEFICIT/GDP

This means that, in order to maintain a stable debt-to-GDP ratio, the government must run an overall deficit equal to the stock of debt times the rate of growth of nominal GDP.

To derive the government's dynamic long-run budget constraint, (A3) needs to be combined with the government's short-run budget constraint:

(A4)   DEFICIT = i . DEBT + PRIMARY EXPENDITURE − TAX,

where i is the nominal interest rate, TAX is total nominal tax revenues and PRIMARY EXPENDITURE is total nominal government expenditures net of debt service. Thus combining (A3) and (A4) and rearranging gives:

(A4) $(r - g)$ *debt* = *tax − primary expenditure,*

where the lower case italicised variables denotes that they are expressed as a proportion of GDP and the real interest rate, r, is defined as the difference between i and π. This implies that, in order to maintain a stable debt-to-GDP ratio, the government must run a primary surplus which is equal to the product of the debt ratio and the difference between the real interest rates and the real growth rate.

Table A6. **The Government's budget constraint, interest rates and growth**

	1961–69[1]	1970-79	1980-89	1990-93
	Proportion of GDP			
TAX	29.1	33.8	34.8	38.4
PRIMARY EXPENDITURE	26.9	33.1	36.1	40.1
Goods and services	19.5	22.2	22.3	23.6
Transfers	7.5	10.9	13.9	16.5
DEFICIT	–0.2	0.2	4.3	6.0
DEBT (end of period)	12.4[2]	12.5	39.1	60.8
	Per cent			
Real interest rates (r)[3]	2.8	1.1	6.2	7.2
Real growth rates (g)	5.3	4.6	3.0	0.2
r – g	–2.5	–3.5	3.2	7.0

1. Starts in 1961 instead of 1960 due to data availability.
2. Constructing a consistent set of consolidated stock and flow accounts is a difficult task and problems invariably exist with the data. Of particular importance is the fact that the consolidated government deficit figures do not cumulate exactly to the reported levels of consolidated net government debt. As a result, the accounting identities discussed in the text do not in fact hold exactly in the data. However, while it is important to be aware of these limitations of the data, they are not serious enough to compromise the historical analysis.
3. The real interest rate is measured as the average bond yield on over 10-year Government of Canada bonds less the year-over-year growth in the GDP price deflator.
Source: "Some macroeconomic implications of rising levels of government debt", *Bank of Canada Review*, Winter 1994/95.

It is possible to analyse the historical deterioration in the debt position in Canada in terms of expression (A4).[1] Averages for the past three decades of the variables in this expression show that the difference between interest rates and the growth rate turned positive in the 1980s, so raising debt costs (see Table A6). Thus, a constant debt-to-GDP ratio could only be maintained if taxes were increased relative to primary expenditures. However, in practice, although both taxes and expenditure rose as a proportion of GDP, primary expenditures increased by more than taxes, largely due to an increase in government transfers to the private sector. Thus, the combined effect of increased debt service costs and lower taxes net of transfers resulted in a series of large deficits and a continual rise in the debt ratio throughout the 1980s and 1990s.

Alternatively, the government's dynamic budget constraint (A4) can also be re-arranged to calculate the steady-state ratio of the primary balance to GDP required to hold the debt-to-GDP ratio at its current level, for given assumptions about the real growth rate and real interest rate, as is done in Table 11 and discussed in the main text in the fiscal policy section.

The effects of fiscal consolidation

This section describes further details of the macroeconometric model simulations briefly discussed in the main text, which have been carried out in order to provide some

144

tentative quantitative guidance as to the scale of the potential long-term benefits from fiscal consolidation in relation to the short-term contractionary effects on the economy. For this purpose an empirical relationship for real long-term interest rates has been incorporated into the OECD Secretariat's INTERLINK macroeconometric model of the Canadian economy. This relationship is based on recent research by the OECD Secretariat as is described more fully in Annex III. The important feature of this relationship as regards the present simulation analysis is that a reduction in the government budget deficit by the equivalent of 1 percentage point of GDP eventually reduces real long-term interest rates by about 15 basis points in the long-run.

A number of variants of the same basic model simulation are considered, namely that of a sustained reduction in government current expenditures by the equivalent of 1 per cent of GDP using a feedback rule for short-term interest rates which respond to target the inflation rate (thus a fall in the inflation rate is followed by an easing of monetary conditions).

The first variant simulation assumes that there is no change in real long-term interest rates despite the fiscal consolidation. In this case, the lower government expenditures lead to a temporary reduction in GDP, although the fall in inflation and consequent easing of short-term rates mean that the magnitude of the decline in GDP is quite modest (the maximum multiplier effect is only about 0.6), see the top panel of Table A7. By the end of the ten year simulation horizon the combination of fiscal contraction and monetary easing has had virtually no aggregate effect on the economy: GDP and inflation are close to their baseline values and even the cumulative deviation of GDP from the baseline (summing all positive and negative deviations over the ten year horizon) is practically zero.

The second variant utilises the estimated relationship for real-long term interest rates discussed above, so that fiscal consolidation leads to a gradual decline in these rates as a result of improvements in the governments budget balance as well as the current account balance. The impact effect of fiscal consolidation is much the same as in the first variant simulation, with declines in both GDP and inflation (see the second panel of Table A7). However, the gradual reduction in real long-term interest rates has a beneficial supply-side effect on the economy by lowering the real user-cost of capital and so stimulating increased investment in productive capacity.[2] Consequently GDP rises above the baseline by the fourth year of the simulation, although it is not until the seventh year of the simulation that the cumulative output loss incurred during the first three years of the simulation is made up. However, beyond this point, fiscal consolidation has a clearly beneficial effect on macroeconomic performance as a consequence of the reduction in the risk premium.

A final "full credibility" variant of the simulation assumes that real interest rates immediately fall by the full amount observed at the end of the previous simulation. In this case, the delay before there are positive effects on GDP is further reduced: GDP is above the baseline after only three years, and by the fifth year the cumulative output loss of the first two years has been made good (see the final panel of Table A7).

145

Table A7. **Simulations of a reduction in government current expenditure by the equivalent of 1 per cent of GDP[1]**

	Year					
	1	2	3	5	7	10
1. No change in real long-term rates						
GDP (per cent)	–0.6	–0.6	–0.3	0.3	0.4	0.1
Cumulative GDP (per cent point years)	–0.6	–1.2	–1.6	–1.2	–0.4	0.0
Inflation (per cent per annum)	–0.1	–0.3	–0.5	–0.6	–0.3	–0.2
Real short-term interest rates (per cent)	–0.9	–0.9	–1.5	–0.8	–0.3	–0.6
Primary budget balance (per cent of GDP)	0.6	0.3	0.2	0.3	0.5	0.3
Total budget balance (per cent of GDP)	0.9	0.9	1.4	1.8	2.1	2.4
2. Lagged fall in real long-term rates						
GDP (per cent)	–0.6	–0.6	–0.2	0.5	0.6	0.3
Cumulative GDP (per cent point years)	–0.6	–1.2	–1.5	–0.8	0.3	1.5
Inflation (per cent per annum)	–0.1	–0.3	–0.5	–0.6	–0.4	–0.3
Real short-term interest rates (per cent)	–0.9	–0.9	–1.6	–1.0	–0.5	–0.7
Real long-term interest rates (per cent)	–0.2	–0.2	–0.4	–0.3	–0.3	–0.4
Primary budget balance (per cent of GDP)	0.6	0.3	0.3	0.3	0.5	0.3
Total budget balance (per cent of GDP)	0.9	1.0	1.6	2.0	2.4	2.8
3. Immediate fall in long-term rates						
GDP (per cent)	–0.6	–0.5	0.0	0.8	0.6	0.3
Cumulative GDP (per cent point years)	–0.6	–1.1	–1.0	0.2	1.5	2.4
Inflation (per cent per annum)	–0.0	–0.4	–0.7	–0.7	–0.3	–0.3
Real short-term interest rates (per cent)	–1.0	–1.4	–1.9	–0.6	–0.7	–0.7
Real long-term interest rates (per cent)	–0.4	–0.4	–0.4	–0.4	–0.4	–0.4
Primary budget balance (per cent of GDP)	0.6	0.3	0.2	0.4	0.5	0.2
Total budget balance (per cent of GDP)	1.0	1.2	1.8	2.3	2.6	2.9

1. All simulations are carried out on the OECD Secretariat's INTERLINK macro model for Canada. Results are expressed as differences from a baseline projection.
Source: OECD Secretariat.

Notes

1. The discussion in this paragraph draws heavily on "Some Macroeconomic Implications of Rising Levels of Government Debt", *Bank of Canada Review*, Winter 1994/95.

2. For a description of the supply-side effects of the lower user-cost of capital in the INTERLINK model see "The Role of Real and Nominal Rigidities in Macroeconomic Adjustment: A Comparative Study of the G3 Economies" by D. Turner, P. Richardson and S. Rauffet, *OECD Economic Studies No.21*, Winter 1993.

Annex VI

Chronology of economic events

1994

January

The governments of Ontario and Quebec sign an agreement committing them to remove trade barriers in construction contracting and labour mobility.

The Bank of Canada's discount rate falls to below 4 per cent, the lowest level in 30 years.

February

The federal government tables its 1994/95 budget calling for a decline in the deficit to C\$ 39.7 billion from an estimated outcome of C\$ 45.7 billion in 1993/94. Specific measures include the closure of military bases and military spending cuts over five years; the freeze of public service wages for another two years; the tightening of eligibility requirements for unemployment benefits; the elimination of capital gains exemptions; and cuts in the business entertainment tax deduction.

The Alberta government budget calls for spending cuts of the order of C\$ 1 billion – including the areas of health, welfare and education – to bring the deficit down to C\$ 1½ billion in 1994/95.

The federal, Quebec, New Brunswick and Ontario governments slash cigarette taxes in an effort to reduce smuggling.

March

The commercial banks raise their prime lending rate to 6¼ per cent.

The Newfoundland budget calls for a sharp reduction in the deficit in 1994/95, and a balanced budget by 1995/96.

April

Banks increase their prime lending rate to 6¾ per cent.

The Manitoba budget calls for a gradual fall in the deficit, with limited spending cuts and higher gambling revenues.

The British Columbia government imposes a C$ 2 billion tax on forestry companies to finance a provincial job creation programme.

The federal government announces a C$ 2 billion five-year aid programme for Atlantic fishermen and related plant workers, covering about 30 000 people.

May

The Quebec budget calls for a slight decline in the deficit to C$ 4½ billion in 1994/95, combining modest spending cuts with tax breaks and new fiscal incentives.

The Ontario budget aims at lowering the deficit from C$ 9½ billion in 1993/94 to C$ 8½ billion in 1994/95, with limited spending cuts and tax reductions.

June

Banks raise their prime lending rate to 8 per cent.

July

The federal and provincial governments signed an agreement to ease internal trade barriers from July 1995.

Banks reduce their prime lending rate in two steps to 7½ per cent.

August

The trade dispute between Canada and the United States over softwood lumber exports was settled in Canada's favour by an extraordinary challenge committee under the terms of the Free Trade Agreement. The US government is expected to refund countervailing duties collected from Canadian companies since 1992.

Banks reduce their prime lending rate to 7¼ per cent.

September

Banks reduce their prime lending rate to 7 per cent.

December

Banks raise the prime lending rate in two ½ point steps to 8 per cent.

The Quebec Premier unveils plans to make Quebec an independent nation within two years based on legislation that would be adopted by the provincial Parliament and ratified in a referendum.

1995

January

Banks raise the prime lending rate in two steps to 9¼ per cent.

February

The federal government delivers its budget, projecting a deficit of C$ 32.7 billion in 1995/96, following a C$ 37.9 billion in 1994/95. Spending cuts of C$ 20 billion over three years are announced including a 60 per cent reduction in business subsidies, the elimination of 45 000 civil servant jobs and a reduction in transfers to the provinces.

Moody's Credit rating agency announced that it would be reviewing the rating of federal government debt, causing the dollar to fall.

The Saskatchewan budget forecasts a C$ 120 million surplus in 1994/95 followed by a C$ 24 million surplus in 1995/96, with cuts in corporate tax and a freeze on total spending.

Alberta tabled its budget, projecting a deficit of C$ 506 million in 1995/96 following a surplus of C$ 110 million in 1994/95. Measures include a cut in programme spending of C$ 478 million, with a cut of C$ 276 million in health spending, and the elimination of 2 000 civil service jobs.

The New Brunswick budget projects a surplus of C$ 68 million on the basis of spending cuts of C$ 93 million, mainly in administration costs, and a reduction in business taxes.

March

The budget in Manitoba forecasts a fiscal surplus of C$ 48 million in 1995/96, with a 2 per cent increase in government spending, an increase in revenue from the lottery fund and a freeze on major taxes.

Banks raise the prime lending rate to 9¾ per cent.

Newfoundland tabled a balanced budget with expectations of increased tax revenues from rising employment.

Prince Edward Island introduced a balanced budget on the basis of spending cuts and a rise in cigarette taxes.

British Columbia presented a balanced budget.

The dispute between Canada and the European Union over fishing quotas of turbot in the Northwest Atlantic reaches a head with a Canadian attack on a Spanish fishing vessel.

April

The Nova Scotia budget projected a deficit of C$ 28 million for 1995/96 with a planned reduction in programme spending of C$ 106 million.

Moody's Credit rating agency downgrade federal government debt, cutting the domestic currency rating to AA1 from AAA and the foreign currency debt to AA2 from AA1.

May

Banks lower the prime lending rate to 9¼ per cent.

The Quebec budget forecast a deficit of C$ 3.9 billion and a balanced budget by 1997/98. Measures include higher payroll taxes and a further harmonisation of the Quebec Sales tax with the federal GST.

June

Banks lower the prime lending rate to 8¾ per cent.

The Progressive Conservatives win a comfortable majority in the Ontario provincial elections on a platform to reduce income taxes by 30 per cent in three years, cut social welfare expenditure and eliminate the deficit by 2000/01.

Moody's Credit rating agency lowers its rating of Quebec's long-term debt citing the province's failure to reduce its deficit despite three years of economic growth.

July

The newly-elected provincial government in Ontario presents a budget which projects a deficit of C$ 8.7 billion in 1995/96. Spending cuts of C$ 1.9 billion in the current year are the first round in a series of spending cuts which are expected to lead to a balanced budget in 2000/01. The budget measures include reductions in spending on welfare, job-training programmes, road and transit projects, and business subsidies.

Banks lower the prime lending rate to 8¼ per cent.

August

Banks lower the prime lending rate to 8 per cent.

STATISTICAL ANNEX AND STRUCTURAL INDICATORS

Table A. **Selected background statistics**

	Average 1985-94	1985	1986	1987	1988	1989	1990	1991	1992	1993	1994
A. Percentage changes											
Private consumption[1]	2.7	5.2	4.4	4.4	4.5	3.4	1.0	-1.6	1.3	1.6	3.0
Gross fixed capital formation[1]	4.1	9.5	6.2	10.8	10.3	6.1	-3.5	-2.9	-1.5	0.6	7.2
Public investment[1]	4.1	11.1	-1.6	2.2	3.6	8.8	6.9	4.9	-0.1	0.7	5.7
Private investment[1]	4.1	9.2	7.4	12.0	11.1	5.7	-4.8	-4.0	-1.7	0.5	7.5
Residential[1]	2.7	9.8	13.3	16.4	2.8	4.8	-9.7	-12.5	7.9	-4.2	3.0
Non-residential[1]	4.7	8.9	4.5	9.7	15.8	6.2	-2.4	-0.2	-5.5	2.7	9.4
GDP[1]	2.5	4.8	3.3	4.2	5.0	2.4	-0.2	-1.8	0.8	2.2	4.6
GDP price deflator	2.8	2.6	2.4	4.7	4.6	4.8	3.1	2.9	1.2	1.1	0.6
Industrial production	1.9	5.6	-0.8	4.9	5.3	-0.1	-3.3	-4.2	1.1	4.5	6.5
Employment	1.5	3.0	3.0	2.7	3.2	2.1	0.6	-1.9	-0.6	1.4	2.1
Compensation of employees (current prices)	5.6	7.8	6.7	8.7	9.7	7.9	5.2	2.8	2.4	1.7	3.0
Productivity (real GDP/employment)	0.9	1.7	0.3	1.4	1.7	0.4	-0.8	0.1	1.3	0.8	2.4
Unit labour costs (compensation/real GDP)	3.0	2.9	3.3	4.4	4.5	5.3	5.5	4.6	1.6	-0.5	-1.5
B. Percentage ratios											
Gross fixed capital formation as per cent of GDP at constant prices	21.6	19.5	20.1	21.4	22.4	23.2	22.5	22.2	21.7	21.4	21.9
Stockbuilding as per cent of GDP at constant prices	0.2	0.4	0.5	0.6	0.5	0.7	-0.3	-0.4	-0.7	0.2	0.5
Foreign balance as per cent of GDP at constant prices	-1.1	1.7	0.9	0.1	-1.1	-2.6	-2.1	-2.7	-2.2	-1.9	-0.8
Compensation of employees as per cent of GDP at current prices	55.0	53.9	54.3	54.2	54.1	54.3	55.6	56.5	56.7	55.9	54.7
Direct taxes as per cent of household income	15.8	13.7	14.8	15.4	15.8	15.6	17.3	17.0	16.4	16.1	16.2
Household saving as per cent of disposable income	10.1	13.3	10.7	9.2	9.7	10.4	9.7	9.9	10.3	9.6	7.9
Unemployment rate	9.6	10.5	9.6	8.8	7.8	7.5	8.1	10.4	11.3	11.2	10.4
C. Other indicator											
Current balance (billion dollars)	-17.2	-4.5	-10.1	-11.8	-17.1	-22.8	-21.6	-23.6	-21.4	-22.3	-16.3

1. At constant 1986 prices.
Source: OECD.

Table B. **Supply and use of resources**

Million Canadian dollars, current prices

	1985	1986	1987	1988	1989	1990	1991	1992	1993	1994
Private consumption	274 503	297 478	322 769	349 937	378 933	399 319	411 960	422 515	436 542	452 859
Public consumption	95 519	100 129	105 836	114 472	124 108	135 157	144 885	150 390	152 158	150 758
Gross fixed investment	94 198	101 560	116 717	132 790	146 075	141 376	132 001	128 865	128 884	139 192
Final domestic demand	464 220	499 167	545 322	597 199	649 116	675 852	688 846	701 770	717 584	742 809
	(9.1)	(7.5)	(9.2)	(9.5)	(8.7)	(4.1)	(1.9)	(1.9)	(2.3)	(3.5)
Stockbuilding	2 281	2 557	3 071	3 795	3 607	-2 835	-3 235	-3 701	1 103	2 822
	(-0.6)	(0.1)	(0.1)	(0.1)	(0)	(-1.0)	(-0.1)	(-0.1)	(0.7)	(0.2)
Total domestic demand	466 501	501 724	548 393	600 994	652 723	673 017	685 611	698 069	718 687	745 631
	(8.4)	(7.6)	(9.3)	(9.6)	(8.6)	(3.1)	(1.9)	(1.8)	(3.0)	(3.7)
Exports	134 919	138 119	145 416	159 309	163 903	168 917	164 849	181 189	209 370	249 371
Imports	123 388	133 369	140 502	156 384	166 079	171 223	172 805	187 254	212 534	243 756
Foreign balance	11 531	4 750	4 914	2 925	-2 176	-2 306	-7 956	-6 065	-3 164	5 615
	(-0.9)	(-1.4)	(0)	(-0.4)	(-0.8)	(0)	(-0.8)	(0.3)	(0.4)	(1.2)
Statistical discrepancy	-44	-808	-1 710	1 987	201	-1 244	-1 178	-1 882	-2 668	-1 193
GDP (market prices)	477 988	505 666	551 597	605 906	650 748	669 467	676 477	690 122	712 855	750 053
	(7.5)	(5.8)	(9.1)	(9.8)	(7.4)	(2.9)	(1.0)	(2.0)	(3.3)	(5.2)

Note: Figures in parentheses are annual growth rates; for stockbuilding and the foreign balance they are contributions to GDP growth.
Source: CANSIM – Statistics Canada.

Table B. **Supply and use of resources** (*cont'd*)

Million Canadian dollars, 1986 prices

	1985	1986	1987	1988	1989	1990	1991	1992	1993	1994
Private consumption	284 923	297 478	310 453	324 301	335 284	338 717	333 396	337 619	342 858	353 175
Public consumption	98 585	100 129	101 857	106 060	110 331	113 890	116 958	118 126	118 660	116 621
Gross fixed investment	95 624	101 560	112 542	124 105	131 630	126 962	123 236	121 419	122 095	130 933
Final domestic demand	479 132	499 167	524 852	554 466	577 245	579 569	573 590	577 164	583 613	600 729
	(5.6)	(4.2)	(5.1)	(5.6)	(4.1)	(0.4)	(–1.0)	(0.6)	(1.1)	(2.9)
Stockbuilding	2 177	2 557	3 222	2 515	3 778	–1 737	–2 427	–3 766	1 006	2 759
	(–0.3)	(0.1)	(0.1)	(–0.1)	(0.2)	(–1.0)	(–0.1)	(–0.2)	(0.9)	(0.3)
Total domestic demand	481 309	501 724	528 074	556 981	581 023	577 832	571 163	573 398	584 619	603 488
	(5.3)	(4.2)	(5.3)	(5.5)	(4.3)	(–0.5)	(–1.2)	(0.4)	(2.0)	(3.2)
Exports	132 218	138 119	142 942	156 528	157 799	164 312	166 687	179 426	198 093	226 271
Imports	123 935	133 369	142 678	162 385	172 584	175 960	181 831	192 000	208 856	230 874
Foreign balance	8 283	4 750	264	–5 857	–14 785	–11 648	–15 144	–12 574	–10 763	–4 603
	(–0.5)	(–0.7)	(–0.9)	(–1.2)	(–1.6)	(0.6)	(–0.6)	(0.5)	(0.3)	(1.1)
Statistical discrepancy	–155	–808	–1 608	1 834	248	–1 029	–967	–1 519	–2 134	–949
GDP (market prices)	489 437	505 666	526 730	552 958	566 486	565 155	555 052	559 305	571 722	597 936
	(4.8)	(3.3)	(4.2)	(5.0)	(2.4)	(–0.2)	(–1.8)	(0.8)	(2.2)	(4.6)

Note: Figures in parentheses are annual growth rates; for stockbuilding and the foreign balance they are contributions to GDP growth.
Source: CANSIM – Statistics Canada.

Table C. **Industrial production, employment and other business indicators**

Seasonally adjusted

	1990	1991	1992	1993	1994	1994 II	1994 III	1994 IV	1995 I	1995 II
Indices of industrial production (1990 = 100)										
Total	100.0	95.8	96.9	101.2	107.8	106.7	109.5	111.4	112.3	111.7
Durable manufactures	100.0	91.4	92.9	99.4	109.2	107.0	111.3	116.5	118.3	115.9
Non-durable manufactures	100.0	94.6	95.6	97.8	101.2	100.7	102.2	102.9	103.0	102.2
New Residential construction (thousands, annual rates)										
Starts	181.6	156.2	168.3	155.4	154.1	205.5	175.6	139.6	77.2	132.4
Completions[1]	206.2	160.0	173.2	161.8	162.1	148.6	213.9	170.8	104.8	115.9
Under construction[2]	100.7	95.0	87.5	79.8	71.6	89.1	79.5	71.6	64.6	68.5
Employment and unemployment (thousands, monthly averages)										
Civilian labour force	14 328	14 408	14 481	14 666	14 832	14 808	14 871	14 895	14 928	14 914
Non-agricultural employment	12 724	12 458	12 403	12 563	12 866	12 824	12 922	13 008	13 049	13 067
Employment[3]										
Mining	152	145	129	120	130	132	137	131	125	132
Manufacturing	1 885	1 692	1 599	1 597	1 632	1 647	1 678	1 644	1 607	1 687
Durables	1 005	885	851	839	879	888	903	893	878	919
Non-durables	880	806	748	758	753	759	775	750	729	768
Transportation, communication and other utilities[4]	902	860	852	841	850	861	862	856	827	849
Unemployment (thousands)	1 166	1 493	1 638	1 648	1 540	1 574	1 513	1 447	1 443	1 420
Unemployment (percentage of civilian labour force)	8.1	10.4	11.3	11.3	10.4	10.6	10.2	9.7	9.7	9.5
Average weekly hours worked in manufacturing	38.2	37.9	38.3	38.6	38.8	38.9	38.8	38.8	38.9	38.4
Retail sales ($ million, monthly averages)	16 047	15 101	15 421	16 151	17 237	17 134	17 268	17 629	17 617	17 634
Orders and inventories in manufacturing ($ million)										
New orders (monthly averages)[5]	24 641	23 313	23 924	26 107	29 520	28 980	30 359	31 676	32 761	31 799
Unfilled orders (end of period)	26 052	25 247	25 959	29 172	33 505	30 985	32 483	33 505	34 428	33 758
Total inventories (end of period)	45 118	42 319	42 181	44 069	48 406	45 733	46 954	48 406	50 872	52 216

1. Not seasonally adjusted.
2. Not seasonally adjusted, end of period.
3. Estimates of employment, earnings and hours from April 1983 are based on a revised survey and are not seasonally adjusted.
4. Includes storage, electric power gas and water utilities.
5. 3-month averages for quarters.
Source: OECD, *Main Economic Indicators*; CANSIM – Statistics Canada.

Table D. Prices, wages and finance

	1990	1991	1992	1993	1994	1994 II	1994 III	1994 IV	1995 I	1995 II
Prices (1985 = 100)										
Consumer prices, all items	100.0	105.6	107.2	109.2	109.4	108.9	109.5	109.8	111.0	111.8
of which:										
Food	100.0	104.8	104.3	106.1	106.6	106.4	106.7	106.7	108.9	109.9
Non-food	100.0	105.8	107.8	109.8	110.0	109.5	110.1	110.5	111.4	112.2
Producer prices, manufactured goods	100.0	99.0	99.5	102.8	108.6	107.5	109.6	111.8	116.1	117.1
Wages and profits										
Hourly earnings in manufacturing (1990 = 100)	100.0	104.8	108.4	110.6	112.4	112.4	111.4	113.0	113.4	113.5
Corporate profits before tax ($ million, annual rates)	44 814	34 829	35 060	42 135	57 357	55 400	59 640	63 380	65 572	63 700
Banking ($ million, end of period)										
Chartered banks:										
Canadian dollar deposits	297 995	311 952	339 085	377 231	406 350	393 667	398 604	406 350	404 720	414 390
of which:										
Personal savings deposits	202 597	216 515	228 732	263 766	280 291	273 169	276 449	280 291	286 450	289 789
Liquid assets	32 099	46 535	57 865	82 181	87 238	78 426	79 457	87 238	88 309	86 526
Holdings of Government of Canada direct and guaranteed securities	6 488	11 819	17 388	32 829	42 291	34 421	37 481	42 291	42 112	42 847
Total loans	290 814	305 814	323 996	357 878	393 064	382 459	384 226	393 064	399 262	403 234
Currency outside banks	19 099	20 373	22 000	23 683	25 432	24 773	25 153	25 432	26 021	25 889
Interest rates (per cent, end of period)										
Prime corporate paper (3 month)	11.7	7.6	7.3	3.9	7.2	6.6	5.3	7.2	8.4	6.9
Yield of long-term Govt. bonds	10.4	9.1	8.6	7.3	9.2	9.1	9.1	9.2	8.8	8.1
Miscellaneous										
Share prices Toronto stock exchange (1990 = 100)	100.0	101.4	99.5	114.1	125.2	123.0	125.5	122.8	121.4	129.2

Source: OECD, *Main Economic Indicators*; CANSIM – Statistics Canada.

Table E. Balance of payments
Million US dollars

	1990	1991	1992	1993	1994	II	1994 III	IV	1995 I	II
Current account										
Merchandise exports	128 410	126 089	132 176	143 970	163 549	164 488	161 268	182 960	182 524	191 316
Merchandise imports	120 112	122 222	126 406	136 036	151 321	154 112	149 140	162 124	167 108	175 292
Trade balance	8 298	3 869	5 771	7 932	12 227	10 372	12 128	20 836	15 416	16 020
Services, net	-29 847	-27 553	-27 333	-30 591	-29 272	-31 784	-24 160	-28 744	-35 656	-33 116
Travel	-5 792	-6 600	-6 749	-6 105	-4 214	-5 244	2 464	-4 612	-8 624	-4 172
Investment income	-19 574	-16 743	-16 545	-20 207	-21 155	-23 120	-22 160	-20 572	-23 348	-25 416
Other services	-4 481	-4 210	-4 039	-4 279	-3 903	-3 420	-4 464	-3 560	-3 684	-3 528
Transfers, net	-63	96	142	339	718	1 188	1 124	140	0	488
Private	955	997	963	1 027	1 067	1 352	1 464	480	752	688
Official	-1 018	-901	-821	-688	-349	-164	-340	-340	-752	-200
Current balance	-21 611	-23 589	-21 420	-22 321	-16 326	-20 220	-10 908	-7 764	-20 244	-16 604
Capital account										
Long-term capital, net	10 455	11 205	8 659	19 957	9 032	7 404	31 684	-25 024	-1 012	30 372
Private, direct	3 120	-2 905	773	-824	1 253	708	328	1 768	3 572	4 388
Private, portfolio	8 569	15 666	9 288	21 003	9 164	8 304	32 244	-24 832	-3 708	27 108
Public[1]	-1 233	-1 557	-1 402	-222	-1 385	-1 612	-888	-1 960	-880	-1 124
Short-term capital, net	13 121	12 527	5 831	8 998	3 206	15 460	-28 324	28 808	41 708	-29 336
Private non-monetary	8 016	6 278	9 091	773	584	764	-4 408	-1 012	15 508	9 096
Private monetary institutions	2 198	4 208	-4 913	-313	633	-3 596	-2 892	22 144	18 088	-29 528
Official non-monetary	2 907	2 041	1 653	8 538	1 989	18 292	-21 024	7 676	8 112	-8 904
Miscellaneous official accounts	0	1	-2	0	-3	-8	0	0	4	4
Errors and omissions	-1 406	-2 611	1 153	-7 099	2 898	-1 164	21 944	-9 456	-12 156	16 064
Change in reserves	557	-2 469	-5 780	-463	-1 194	1 472	14 392	-13 440	8 300	496

1. Excludes special transactions.
Source: Statistics Canada; OECD Secretariat.

159

Table F. **Public sector**

	A. Budget indicators: general government accounts *(Per cent of GDP)*[1]				
	1960	1970	1980	1993	1994
Current receipts	26.0	34.3	36.1	42.1	41.9
Non-interest expenditure	26.1	31.2	34.9	41.6	39.4
Primary budget balance	–0.6	1.9	–0.9	–2.2	–0.2
Net interest payments	1.1	1.1	1.9	5.0	5.1
General government budget balance	–1.7	0.8	–2.8	–7.3	–5.3
of which:					
Federal	–0.6	0.3	–3.4	–4.9	–3.8
Provincial, local, hospitals	–1.1	–0.8	–0.3	–2.2	–1.2
Pension plans[2]	0.0	1.3	1.0	–0.1	–0.2
General government debt					
Gross debt	73.8*	63.0	57.4	105.9	107.9
Net debt	26.7*	11.6	13.3	61.9	64.4
of which:					
Federal	18.9	7.3	16.0	52.2	53.0

	B. The structure of expenditure *(per cent of GDP)*				
Total general government					
expenditure	28.8	34.9	40.3	50.8	48.5
Current consumption	13.4	18.5	19.1	21.3	20.1
Transfers to persons	7.8	7.8	9.8	15.8	15.1
Subsidies (+ capital assistance)	0.8	1.1	3.0	1.8	1.6
Capital formation	3.8	3.5	2.7	2.2	2.2
Other programme expenditure	0.2	0.3	0.3	0.4	0.3
Total programme expenditure	26.0	31.2	34.9	41.0	39.4
Gross interest payments	2.8	3.6	5.4	9.2	9.1

	C. General government expenditure by function, financial management system basis *(per cent of GDP, fiscal year)*				
	1965-66	1970-71	1980-81	1990-91	1991-92
Social services	5.4	6.7	8.6	10.2	11.7
Education	5.2	6.8	5.8	5.8	6.3
Health	2.9	4.8	5.2	6.2	6.7
Transport and Communication	3.7	3.1	3.0	2.3	2.3
National Defence	2.7	2.0	1.6	1.7	1.6
General Services	1.7	2.6	2.8	2.7	2.8

* 1961.
1. National accounts basis.
2. Canada and Quebec Pension Plans.
Source: Department of Finance.

160

Table G. **Financial markets**

	1970	1980	1992	1993
Size of the financial sector (percentages)[1]				
Sector employment/total employment	4.8	5.7	6.2	5.9
Net financial assets/GDP	6.3	4.3	7.5	6.1
Structure of financial assets and liabilities				
Financial institutions' share in domestic				
financial assets (per cent)	33.1	38.6	41.5	42.0
Government securities in NFB[2] total financial				
assets (per cent)	0.3	0.1	2.2	2.6
Structure of NFB liabilities				
Debt to equity ratio[3]	1.17	1.42	1.48	1.50
Short-term:				
Securities and mortgages ($ billion)	8.7	33.4	118.9	121.0
Trade payables ($ billion)	12.4	54.9	101.6	108.2
Long-term:				
Bonds ($ billion)	13.7	28.7	97.5	106.6
Loans and corporate claims ($ billion)	27.0	105.5	252.5	274.2
Internationalisation of markets				
Share of foreign currency assets and liabilities				
in the banking sector[4]				
Assets	28.9	39.1	30.8	31.9
Liabilities	28.6	40.2	33.3	34.4
Foreign purchases of Canadian securities[5]	12.4	18.2	75.4	48.5
Canadian purchases of foreign securities[5]	–1.2	0.6	20.8	19.1
Debt (per cent of GDP)				
Private non-financial sector				
NFB[2, 6]	77.3	81.6	87.8	89.8
Households[7]	45.3	52.5	63.2	63.4

1. Public and private financial institutions and insurance.
2. NFB = non-financial corporate business, excluding farms.
3. (Liabilities-shares)/shares.
4. Per cent of consolidated balance sheet of chartered banks, excludes other deposit-taking institutions.
5. Per cent of net issues on domestic securities markets. Data include new issues as well as secondary market transactions.
6. Liabilities less shares.
7. Persons and unincorporated business liabilities less trade payables, other loans and other Canadian bonds.
Source : *Bank of Canada Review;* Labour Force Survey; National Authorities (National Balance Sheet; Security transactions with non-residents).

Table H. **Labour market indicators**

	A. Labour market performance			
	Cyclical peak 1979	Cyclical trough 1982	1985	1994
Standardised unemployment rate	7.4	10.9	10.6	10.5
Unemployment rate:				
Total	7.5	11.0	10.5	10.4
Male	6.7	11.1	10.4	10.8
Woman	8.7	10.8	10.7	9.9
Youth[1]	12.8	18.6	16.3	16.5
Share of long-term unemployment in total unemployment[2]	3.7	5.1	10.1	14.8
Dispersion of regional unemployment rates[3]	3.4	3.0	3.8	4.2

	B. Structural or institutional characteristics			
	1970	1980	1985	1994*
Participation rate:[4]				
Total	62.4	71.8	74.0	75.0
Male	84.5	85.9	84.7	82.2
Women	40.4	57.8	63.2	67.8
Employment/population (15-64 years)	66.0	66.4	66.1	67.1
Average hours worked	36.0	35.2	34.8	34.9
Part-time work				
(as per cent of dependent employment)	n.a.	12.8	15.4	17.0
Non-wage labour costs[5]				
(as percentage of total compensation)	6.1	8.5	9.8	12.7
Government unemployment insurance				
replacement ratio[6]	22.5	31.2	33.8	29.5
Unionisation rate[7]	36.4	37.6	39.0	37.5

	Average percentage changes (annual rates)		
	1970/1960	1980/1970	1994*/1980
Labour force	2.7	3.3	1.5
Employment:			
Total	2.9	3.1	1.3
Goods-producing	0.6	1.8	−0.4
Services	4.3	4.1	2.1

*   Or latest available year.
1.   People between 15 and 24 years as a percentage of the labour force of the same age group.
2.   People looking for a job since one year or more.
3.   Measured by standard deviation for 10 provinces.
4.   Labour force as a percentage of relevant population group, aged between 15 and 64 years.
5.   Employers' contributions to social security and pension funds.
6.   Unemployment benefits per unemployed divided by the compensation per employee.
7.   Figures for 1970 are 1970-79 average.
Source :   CANSIM – Statistics Canada; Canadian Authorities; OECD Secretariat.

Table I. **Production structure and performance indicators**

| | A. Production structure | | | | | |
| | Per cent share of GDP at factor cost (constant prices) | | | Per cent share of total employment | | |
	1975	1980	1993	1975	1980	1993
Agriculture	2.8	2.4	2.3	5.2	4.5	3.6
Mining and quarrying	5.4	4.5	4.2	1.5	1.8	1.2
Manufacturing	20.4	19.7	17.8	20.2	19.7	14.5
of which:						
Food and beverages	2.3	2.3	1.8	2.5	2.4	1.9
Paper and paper products	1.8	2.0	1.5	1.4	1.3	1.0
Primary metal industries	1.9	1.4	1.5	1.3	1.3	0.8
Fabricated metal products, machinery						
and equipment	4.7	4.7	4.8	4.6		
Chemicals and chemical products	1.2	1.3	1.5	0.9	1.0	0.8
Construction	6.4	6.4	5.3	6.5	5.8	5.3
Market services	57.7	59.2	63.0	58.7	60.2	67.6
of which:						
Transport, storage and communication	7.4	7.8	8.5	7.6	7.3	6.2
Wholesale and retail trade	11.3	10.7	12.1	17.6	17.2	17.3
Finance, insurance and real estate	13.6	14.9	16.9	5.1	5.7	6.2
Community, business social and personal						
services	22.3	22.4	22.3	27.2	28.9	36.8
Government services	8.1	7.4	6.5	7.2	6.9	6.9

| | B. Manufacturing sector performance *(constant prices)* | | |
| | *Productivity growth by sector (GDP/employment, annual rate)* | | |
	1980/1975	1990/1980	1993/1980
Manufacturing	0.4	2.7	2.8
of which:			
Food and beverages	1.4	1.8	1.4
Paper and paper products	3.6	0.9	1.4
Primary metal industries	−5.4	2.8	5.3
Chemicals and chemical products	1.3	4.6	3.9

Source: Canadian authorities; OECD, *National Accounts.*

BASIC STATISTICS:

INTERNATIONAL COMPARISONS

	Units	Reference period [1]	Australia	Austria
Population				
Total	Thousands	1992	17 489	7 884
Inhabitants per sq. km	Number	1992	2	94
Net average annual increase over previous 10 years	%	1992	1.4	0.4
Employment				
Civilian employment (CE)[2]	Thousands	1992	7 637	3 546
Of which: Agriculture	% of CE		5.3	7.1
Industry	% of CE		23.8	35.6
Services	% of CE		71	57.4
Gross domestic product (GDP)				
At current prices and current exchange rates	Bill. US$	1992	296.6	186.2
Per capita	US$		16 959	23 616
At current prices using current PPPs[3]	Bill. US$	1992	294.5	142
Per capita	US$		16 800	18 017
Average annual volume growth over previous 5 years	%	1992	2	3.4
Gross fixed capital formation (GFCF)	% of GDP	1992	19.7	25
Of which: Machinery and equipment	% of GDP		9.3	9.9
Residential construction	% of GDP		5.1	5.7
Average annual volume growth over previous 5 years	%	1992	−1	5.1
Gross saving ratio[4]	% of GDP	1992	15.6	25.1
General government				
Current expenditure on goods and services	% of GDP	1992	18.5	18.4
Current disbursements[5]	% of GDP	1992	36.9	46.2
Current receipts	% of GDP	1992	33.1	48.3
Net official development assistance	% of GNP	1992	0.33	0.3
Indicators of living standards				
Private consumption per capita using current PPPs[3]	US$	1992	10 527	9 951
Passenger cars, per 1 000 inhabitants	Number	1990	430	382
Telephones, per 1 000 inhabitants	Number	1990	448	589
Television sets, per 1 000 inhabitants	Number	1989	484	475
Doctors, per 1 000 inhabitants	Number	1991	2	2.1
Infant mortality per 1 000 live births	Number	1991	7.1	7.4
Wages and prices (average annual increase over previous 5 years)				
Wages (earnings or rates according to availability)	%	1992	5	5.4
Consumer prices	%	1992	5.2	3
Foreign trade				
Exports of goods, fob*	Mill. US$	1992	42 844	44 361
As % of GDP	%		14.4	23.8
Average annual increase over previous 5 years	%		10.1	10.4
Imports of goods, cif*	Mill. US$	1992	40 751	54 038
As % of GDP	%		13.7	29
Average annual increase over previous 5 years	%		8.6	10.7
Total official reserves[6]	Mill. SDRs	1992	8 152	9 006
As ratio of average monthly imports of goods	Ratio		2.4	2

* At current prices and exchange rates.
1. Unless otherwise stated.
2. According to the definitions used in OECD *Labour Force Statistics*.
3. PPPs = Purchasing Power Parities.
4. Gross saving = Gross national disposable income minus private and government consumption.
5. Current disbursements = Current expenditure on goods and services plus current transfers and payments of property income.
6. Gold included in reserves is valued at 35 SDRs per ounce. End of year.
7. Including Luxembourg.

EMPLOYMENT OPPORTUNITIES

Economics Department, OECD

The Economics Department of the OECD offers challenging and rewarding opportunities to economists interested in applied policy analysis in an international environment. The Department's concerns extend across the entire field of economic policy analysis, both macroeconomic and microeconomic. Its main task is to provide, for discussion by committees of senior officials from Member countries, documents and papers dealing with current policy concerns. Within this programme of work, three major responsibilities are:

- to prepare regular surveys of the economies of individual Member countries;
- to issue full twice-yearly reviews of the economic situation and prospects of the OECD countries in the context of world economic trends;
- to analyse specific policy issues in a medium-term context for the OECD as a whole, and to a lesser extent for the non-OECD countries.

The documents prepared for these purposes, together with much of the Department's other economic work, appear in published form in the *OECD Economic Outlook, OECD Economic Surveys, OECD Economic Studies* and the Department's *Working Papers* series.

The Department maintains a world econometric model, INTERLINK, which plays an important role in the preparation of the policy analyses and twice-yearly projections. The availability of extensive cross-country data bases and good computer resources facilitates comparative empirical analysis, much of which is incorporated into the model.

The Department is made up of about 80 professional economists from a variety of backgrounds and Member countries. Most projects are carried out by small teams and last from four to eighteen months. Within the Department, ideas and points of view are widely discussed; there is a lively professional interchange, and all professional staff have the opportunity to contribute actively to the programme of work.

Skills the Economics Department is looking for:

a) Solid competence in using the tools of both microeconomic and macroeconomic theory to answer policy questions. Experience indicates that this normally requires the equivalent of a Ph.D. in economics or substantial relevant professional experience to compensate for a lower degree.

b) Solid knowledge of economic statistics and quantitative methods; this includes how to identify data, estimate structural relationships, apply basic techniques of time series analysis, and test hypotheses. It is essential to be able to interpret results sensibly in an economic policy context.

c) A keen interest in and extensive knowledge of policy issues, economic developments and their political/social contexts.

d) Interest and experience in analysing questions posed by policy-makers and presenting the results to them effectively and judiciously. Thus, work experience in government agencies or policy research institutions is an advantage.

e) The ability to write clearly, effectively, and to the point. The OECD is a bilingual organisation with French and English as the official languages. Candidates must have excellent knowledge of one of these languages, and some knowledge of the other. Knowledge of other languages might also be an advantage for certain posts.

f) For some posts, expertise in a particular area may be important, but a successful candidate is expected to be able to work on a broader range of topics relevant to the work of the Department. Thus, except in rare cases, the Department does not recruit narrow specialists.

g) The Department works on a tight time schedule with strict deadlines. Moreover, much of the work in the Department is carried out in small groups. Thus, the ability to work with other economists from a variety of cultural and professional backgrounds, to supervise junior staff, and to produce work on time is important.

General information

The salary for recruits depends on educational and professional background. Positions carry a basic salary from FF 305 700 or FF 377 208 for Administrators (economists) and from FF 438 348 for Principal Administrators (senior economists). This may be supplemented by expatriation and/or family allowances, depending on nationality, residence and family situation. Initial appointments are for a fixed term of two to three years.

Vacancies are open to candidates from OECD Member countries. The Organisation seeks to maintain an appropriate balance between female and male staff and among nationals from Member countries.

For further information on employment opportunities in the Economics Department, contact:

Administrative Unit
Economics Department
OECD
2, rue André-Pascal
75775 PARIS CEDEX 16
FRANCE

E-Mail: compte.esadmin@oecd.org

Applications citing ''ECSUR'', together with a detailed *curriculum vitae* in English or French, should be sent to the Head of Personnel at the above address.

MAIN SALES OUTLETS OF OECD PUBLICATIONS
PRINCIPAUX POINTS DE VENTE DES PUBLICATIONS DE L'OCDE

ARGENTINA – ARGENTINE
Carlos Hirsch S.R.L.
Galería Güemes, Florida 165, 4° Piso
1333 Buenos Aires   Tel. (1) 331.1787 y 331.2391
Telefax: (1) 331.1787

AUSTRALIA – AUSTRALIE
D.A. Information Services
648 Whitehorse Road, P.O.B 163
Mitcham, Victoria 3132   Tel. (03) 9873.4411
Telefax: (03) 9873.5679

AUSTRIA – AUTRICHE
Gerold & Co.
Graben 31
Wien I   Tel. (0222) 533.50.14
Telefax: (0222) 512.47.31.29

BELGIUM – BELGIQUE
Jean De Lannoy
Avenue du Roi 202 Koningslaan
B-1060 Bruxelles   Tel. (02) 538.51.69/538.08.41
Telefax: (02) 538.08.41

CANADA
Renouf Publishing Company Ltd.
1294 Algoma Road
Ottawa, ON K1B 3W8   Tel. (613) 741.4333
Telefax: (613) 741.5439
Stores:
61 Sparks Street
Ottawa, ON K1P 5R1   Tel. (613) 238.8985
211 Yonge Street
Toronto, ON M5B 1M4   Tel. (416) 363.3171
Telefax: (416)363.59.63

Les Éditions La Liberté Inc.
3020 Chemin Sainte-Foy
Sainte-Foy, PQ G1X 3V6   Tel. (418) 658.3763
Telefax: (418) 658.3763

Federal Publications Inc.
165 University Avenue, Suite 701
Toronto, ON M5H 3B8   Tel. (416) 860.1611
Telefax: (416) 860.1608

Les Publications Fédérales
1185 Université
Montréal, QC H3B 3A7   Tel. (514) 954.1633
Telefax: (514) 954.1635

CHINA – CHINE
China National Publications Import ·
Export Corporation (CNPIEC)
16 Gongti E. Road, Chaoyang District
P.O. Box 88 or 50
Beijing 100704 PR   Tel. (01) 506.6688
Telefax: (01) 506.3101

CHINESE TAIPEI – TAIPEI CHINOIS
Good Faith Worldwide Int'l. Co. Ltd.
9th Floor, No. 118, Sec. 2
Chung Hsiao E. Road
Taipei   Tel. (02) 391.7396/391.7397
Telefax: (02) 394.9176

CZECH REPUBLIC – RÉPUBLIQUE TCHÈQUE
Artia Pegas Press Ltd.
Narodni Trida 25
POB 825
111 21 Praha 1   Tel. (2) 2 46 04
Telefax: (2) 2 78 72

DENMARK – DANEMARK
Munksgaard Book and Subscription Service
35, Nørre Søgade, P.O. Box 2148
DK-1016 København K   Tel. (33) 12.85.70
Telefax: (33) 12.93.87

EGYPT – ÉGYPTE
Middle East Observer
41 Sherif Street
Cairo   Tel. 392.6919
Telefax: 360-6804

FINLAND – FINLANDE
Akateeminen Kirjakauppa
Keskuskatu 1, P.O. Box 128
00100 Helsinki

Subscription Services/Agence d'abonnements :
P.O. Box 23
00371 Helsinki   Tel. (358 0) 121 4416
Telefax: (358 0) 121.4450

FRANCE
OECD/OCDE
Mail Orders/Commandes par correspondance:
2, rue André-Pascal
75775 Paris Cedex 16   Tel. (33-1) 45.24.82.00
Telefax: (33-1) 49.10.42.76
Telex: 640048 OCDE
Internet: Compte.PUBSINQ @ oecd.org
Orders via Minitel, France only/
Commandes par Minitel, France exclusivement :
36 15 OCDE

OECD Bookshop/Librairie de l'OCDE :
33, rue Octave-Feuillet
75016 Paris   Tel. (33-1) 45.24.81.81
(33-1) 45.24.81.67
Dawson
B.P. 40
91121 Palaiseau Cedex   Tel. 69.10.47.00
Telefax : 64.54.83.26

Documentation Française
29, quai Voltaire
75007 Paris   Tel. 40.15.70.00
Economica
49 rue Héricart
75015 Paris   Tel. 45.78.12.92
Telefax : 40.58.15.70
Gibert Jeune (Droit-Économie)
6, place Saint-Michel
75006 Paris   Tel. 43.25.91.19
Librairie du Commerce International
10, avenue d'Iéna
75016 Paris   Tel. 40.73.34.60
Librairie Dunod
Université Paris-Dauphine
Place du Maréchal de Lattre de Tassigny
75016 Paris   Tel. 44.05.40.13
Librairie Lavoisier
11, rue Lavoisier
75008 Paris   Tel. 42.65.39.95
Librairie des Sciences Politiques
30, rue Saint-Guillaume
75007 Paris   Tel. 45.48.36.02
P.U.F.
49, boulevard Saint-Michel
75005 Paris   Tel. 43.25.83.40
Librairie de l'Université
12a, rue Nazareth
13100 Aix-en-Provence   Tel. (16) 42.26.18.08
Documentation Française
165, rue Garibaldi
69003 Lyon   Tel. (16) 78.63.32.23
Librairie Decitre
29, place Bellecour
69002 Lyon   Tel. (16) 72.40.54.54
Librairie Sauramps
Le Triangle
34967 Montpellier Cedex 2   Tel. (16) 67.58.85.15
Tekefax: (16) 67.58.27.36
A la Sorbonne Actual
23 rue de l'Hôtel des Postes
06000 Nice   Tel. (16) 93.13.77.75
Telefax: (16) 93.80.75.69

GERMANY – ALLEMAGNE
OECD Publications and Information Centre
August-Bebel-Allee 6
D-53175 Bonn   Tel. (0228) 959.120
Telefax: (0228) 959.12.17

GREECE – GRÈCE
Librairie Kauffmann
Mavrokordatou 9
106 78 Athens   Tel. (01) 32.55.321
Telefax: (01) 32.30.320

HONG-KONG
Swindon Book Co. Ltd.
Astoria Bldg. 3F
34 Ashley Road, Tsimshatsui
Kowloon, Hong Kong   Tel. 2376.2062
Telefax: 2376.0685

HUNGARY – HONGRIE
Euro Info Service
Margitsziget, Európa Ház
1138 Budapest   Tel. (1) 111.62.16
Telefax: (1) 111.60.61

ICELAND – ISLANDE
Mál Mog Menning
Laugavegi 18, Pósthólf 392
121 Reykjavik   Tel. (1) 552.4240
Telefax: (1) 562.3523

INDIA – INDE
Oxford Book and Stationery Co.
Scindia House
New Delhi 110001   Tel. (11) 331.5896/5308
Telefax: (11) 332.5993
17 Park Street
Calcutta 700016   Tel. 240832

INDONESIA – INDONÉSIE
Pdii-Lipi
P.O. Box 4298
Jakarta 12042   Tel. (21) 573.34.67
Telefax: (21) 573.34.67

IRELAND – IRLANDE
Government Supplies Agency
Publications Section
4/5 Harcourt Road
Dublin 2   Tel. 661.31.11
Telefax: 475.27.60

ISRAEL
Praedicta
5 Shatner Street
P.O. Box 34030
Jerusalem 91430   Tel. (2) 52.84.90/1/2
Telefax: (2) 52.84.93
R.O.Y. International
P.O. Box 13056
Tel Aviv 61130   Tel. (3) 546 1423
Telefax: (3) 546 1442
Palestinian Authority/Middle East:
INDEX Information Services
P.O.B. 19502
Jerusalem   Tel. (2) 27.12.19
Telefax: (2) 27.16.34

ITALY – ITALIE
Libreria Commissionaria Sansoni
Via Duca di Calabria 1/1
50125 Firenze   Tel. (055) 64.54.15
Telefax: (055) 64.12.57
Via Bartolini 29
20155 Milano   Tel. (02) 36.50.83
Editrice e Libreria Herder
Piazza Montecitorio 120
00186 Roma   Tel. 679.46.28
Telefax: 678.47.51

Libreria Hoepli
Via Hoepli 5
20121 Milano   Tel. (02) 86.54.46
                   Telefax: (02) 805.28.86

Libreria Scientifica
Dott. Lucio de Biasio 'Aeiou'
Via Coronelli, 6
20146 Milano   Tel. (02) 48.95.45.52
                   Telefax: (02) 48.95.45.48

JAPAN – JAPON
OECD Publications and Information Centre
Landic Akasaka Building
2-3-4 Akasaka, Minato-ku
Tokyo 107   Tel. (81.3) 3586.2016
                   Telefax: (81.3) 3584.7929

KOREA – CORÉE
Kyobo Book Centre Co. Ltd.
P.O. Box 1658, Kwang Hwa Moon
Seoul   Tel. 730.78.91
                   Telefax: 735.00.30

MALAYSIA – MALAISIE
University of Malaya Bookshop
University of Malaya
P.O. Box 1127, Jalan Pantai Baru
59700 Kuala Lumpur
Malaysia   Tel. 756.5000/756.5425
                   Telefax: 756.3246

MEXICO – MEXIQUE
OECD Publications and Information Centre
Edificio INFOTEC
Av. San Fernando no. 37
Col. Toriello Guerra
Tlalpan C.P. 14050
Mexico D.F.
             Tel. (525) 606 00 11 Extension 100
                   Fax : (525) 606 13 07

Revistas y Periodicos Internacionales S.A. de C.V.
Florencia 57 - 1004
Mexico, D.F. 06600   Tel. 207.81.00
                   Telefax: 208.39.79

NETHERLANDS – PAYS-BAS
SDU Uitgeverij Plantijnstraat
Externe Fondsen
Postbus 20014
2500 EA's-Gravenhage   Tel. (070) 37.89.880
Voor bestellingen: Telefax: (070) 34.75.778

**NEW ZEALAND
NOUVELLE-ZÉLANDE**
GPLegislation Services
P.O. Box 12418
Thorndon, Wellington   Tel. (04) 496.5655
                   Telefax: (04) 496.5698

NORWAY – NORVÈGE
Narvesen Info Center – NIC
Bertrand Narvesens vei 2
P.O. Box 6125 Etterstad
0602 Oslo 6   Tel. (022) 57.33.00
                   Telefax: (022) 68.19.01

PAKISTAN
Mirza Book Agency
65 Shahrah Quaid-E-Azam
Lahore 54000   Tel. (42) 353.601
                   Telefax: (42) 231.730

PHILIPPINE – PHILIPPINES
International Booksource Center Inc.
Rm 179/920 Cityland 10 Condo Tower 2
HV dela Costa Ext cor Valero St.
Makati Metro Manila   Tel. (632) 817 9676
                   Telefax : (632) 817 1741

POLAND – POLOGNE
Ars Polona
00-950 Warszawa
Krakowskie Przedmieácie 7   Tel. (22) 264760
                   Telefax : (22) 268673

PORTUGAL
Livraria Portugal
Rua do Carmo 70-74
Apart. 2681
1200 Lisboa   Tel. (01) 347.49.82/5
                   Telefax: (01) 347.02.64

SINGAPORE – SINGAPOUR
Gower Asia Pacific Pte Ltd.
Golden Wheel Building
41, Kallang Pudding Road, No. 04-03
Singapore 1334   Tel. 741.5166
                   Telefax: 742.9356

SPAIN – ESPAGNE
Mundi-Prensa Libros S.A.
Castelló 37, Apartado 1223
Madrid 28001   Tel. (91) 431.33.99
                   Telefax: (91) 575.39.98

Mundi-Prensa Barcelona
Consell de Cent No. 391
08009 – Barcelona   Tel. (93) 488.34.92
                   Telefax: (93) 487.76.59

Llibreria de la Generalitat
Palau Moja
Rambla dels Estudis, 118
08002 – Barcelona
          (Subscripcions) Tel. (93) 318.80.12
          (Publicacions) Tel. (93) 302.67.23
                   Telefax: (93) 412.18.54

SRI LANKA
Centre for Policy Research
c/o Colombo Agencies Ltd.
No. 300-304, Galle Road
Colombo 3   Tel. (1) 574240, 573551-2
                   Telefax: (1) 575394, 510711

SWEDEN – SUÈDE
CE Fritzes AB
S-106 47 Stockholm   Tel. (08) 690.90.90
                   Telefax: (08) 20.50.21

Subscription Agency/Agence d'abonnements :
Wennergren-Williams Info AB
P.O. Box 1305
171 25 Solna   Tel. (08) 705.97.50
                   Telefax: (08) 27.00.71

SWITZERLAND – SUISSE
Maditec S.A. (Books and Periodicals - Livres
et périodiques)
Chemin des Palettes 4
Case postale 266
1020 Renens VD 1   Tel. (021) 635.08.65
                   Telefax: (021) 635.07.80

Librairie Payot S.A.
4, place Pépinet
CP 3212
1002 Lausanne   Tel. (021) 320.25.11
                   Telefax: (021) 320.25.14

Librairie Unilivres
6, rue de Candolle
1205 Genève   Tel. (022) 320.26.23
                   Telefax: (022) 329.73.18

Subscription Agency/Agence d'abonnements :
Dynapresse Marketing S.A.
38 avenue Vibert
1227 Carouge   Tel. (022) 308.07.89
                   Telefax: (022) 308.07.99

See also – Voir aussi :
OECD Publications and Information Centre
August-Bebel-Allee 6
D-53175 Bonn (Germany)   Tel. (0228) 959.120
                   Telefax: (0228) 959.12.17

THAILAND – THAÏLANDE
Suksit Siam Co. Ltd.
113, 115 Fuang Nakhon Rd.
Opp. Wat Rajbopith
Bangkok 10200   Tel. (662) 225.9531/2
                   Telefax: (662) 222.5188

TURKEY – TURQUIE
Kültür Yayinlari Is-Türk Ltd. Sti.
Atatürk Bulvari No. 191/Kat 13
Kavaklidere/Ankara   Tel. 428.11.40 Ext. 2458
Dolmabahce Cad. No. 29
Besiktas/Istanbul   Tel. (312) 260 7188
                   Telex: (312) 418 29 46

UNITED KINGDOM – ROYAUME-UNI
HMSO
Gen. enquiries   Tel. (171) 873 8496
Postal orders only:
P.O. Box 276, London SW8 5DT
Personal Callers HMSO Bookshop
49 High Holborn, London WC1V 6HB
                   Telefax: (171) 873 8416
Branches at: Belfast, Birmingham, Bristol,
Edinburgh, Manchester

UNITED STATES – ÉTATS-UNIS
OECD Publications and Information Center
2001 L Street N.W., Suite 650
Washington, D.C. 20036-4910 Tel. (202) 785.6323
                   Telefax: (202) 785.0350

VENEZUELA
Libreria del Este
Avda F. Miranda 52, Aptdo. 60337
Edificio Galipán
Caracas 106   Tel. 951.1705/951.2307/951.1297
                   Telegram: Libreste Caracas

Subscriptions to OECD periodicals may also be
placed through main subscription agencies.

Les abonnements aux publications périodiques de
l'OCDE peuvent être souscrits auprès des
principales agences d'abonnement.

Orders and inquiries from countries where Distribu-
tors have not yet been appointed should be sent to:
OECD Publications Service, 2 rue André-Pascal,
75775 Paris Cedex 16, France.

Les commandes provenant de pays où l'OCDE n'a
pas encore désigné de distributeur peuvent être
adressées à : OCDE, Service des Publications,
2, rue André-Pascal, 75775 Paris Cedex 16, France.

                                      10-1995

OECD PUBLICATIONS, 2 rue André-Pascal, 75775 PARIS CEDEX 16
PRINTED IN FRANCE
(10 95 01 1) ISBN 92-64-14669-5 - No. 48207 1995
ISSN 0376-6438